VACATION COUN**SELL**ING

LINDA NYY

A NATIONAL PUBLISHERS BOOK
REGENTS/PRENTICE HALL
Upper Saddle River, New Jersey 07458

Library of Congress Cataloging-in-Publication Data

Nyy, Linda.
    Vacation counselling / Linda Nyy.
        p.   cm.
    Includes index.
    ISBN 0-13-945676-7
    1. Travel agents--Vocational guidance.   I. Title.
G154.N98   1989
380.1'459102373--dc19   89-3237
                                                           CIP

Cover and Interior Design: Hudson River Studio
Editing and Production: Ellen Schneid Coleman and Jane Andrassi
Illustrations by Robert Pope
Cover photo, *Fairsky*, courtesy Sitmar Cruises

Printed in the United States of America
10 9 8 7 6 5 4

ISBN   0-13-945676-7

Prentice-Hall International (UK) Limited, London
Prentice-Hall of Australia Pty. Limited, Sydney
Prentice-Hall Canada Inc., Toronto
Prentice-Hall Hispanoamericana, S.A., Mexico
Prentice-Hall of India Private Limited, New Delhi
Prentice-Hall of Japan, Inc., Tokyo
Pearson Education Asia Pte. Ltd., Singapore
Editoria Prentice-Hall do Brasil, Ltda., Rio De Janeiro

<u>THANKS</u>

To my parents, Ed and Bee Nyy, who believe in me, and whose support has enabled me always to reach out for the greatest.

To J. B. Shaw, whose advice about writing has been invaluable for help in editing this manuscript.

To Phil White, whose gift of the computer and friendship without complaints see me through my projects.

CONTENTS

PREFACE

There is an opportunity to make money in vacation travel sales if counsellors are willing to acquire more knowledge about people, destinations, and products. *Vacation CounSELLing* is a guidebook on counselling procedures and techniques for selling vacation travel. It teaches counsellors to be accurate and concise in conversations, thereby selling more in less time. It shows how to sell the right product to the right person, thus eliminating time-consuming problems and gaining more repeat and referral clients.

In order to help counsellors attain these profitable results, *Vacation CounSELLing* constantly focuses on the basics of the interpersonal skills of listening, questioning, communicating with confidence, and keeping the channels of information open.

The book also covers the actual sales process: meeting the client, getting to know the client, matching the products to the client, overcoming the client's objections, and closing the sale. The procedure incorporates the use of tangible aids such as maps, video tapes, and brochures into the sales exchange.

The book then discusses pointers for selling packaged tours and cruises, and on preparing clients for the vacation trip they have chosen. The final part of the book gives tips for handling complaints and for gaining future sales.

The book encourages vacation counsellors to discover how each client is different, and to understand that each client seeks a vacation in order to satisfy an individual emotion, desire, or dream. So, even though there are general guidelines for selling vacations, the counselling career demands distinctive use of professional judgment, discretion, and ethics for the particular sales situation.

With that in mind, it is hoped that this text will make vacation counsellors more knowledgeable about sales and more aware of the people to whom they sell.

1

TRAITS OF THE SUCCESSFUL COUNSELLOR

KEY TERMS
Retail Sales
Vacation Counsellor
Destination Geography
Project-Oriented
Fam

This text concerns itself with retail travel; that is, selling vacation products to individuals as opposed to selling corporate travel to businesspersons or selling vacation, corporate, meeting planning, or incentive travel to groups.

Retail travel products include airline seats, hotel rooms, car rentals, travel insurance, tours, cruises, rail tickets, and, increasingly, services such as travel information and advice.

The person who works in the retail (often called vacation or leisure) segment of an agency is called a retail vacation travel counsellor (or consultant).

Successful vacation travel counsellors are people-oriented individuals. They enjoy interaction. They like conversation. And they usually are thrilled to meet other people of the world, even if they don't speak their language.

Vacation counsellors are also place-oriented people. In addition to actually visiting some countries, they travel vicariously to all the places they sell.

Counsellors usually work in a comfortable office atmosphere, with colorful posters and guidebooks depicting the unique and exciting cultures of the world. They take time to get to know their customers and spend a good portion of their day discussing worldwide adventures with them.

But there is more to a counsellor's work than the opportunity to discuss the beauties of the world hour after hour. There is a difficult side of retail selling. For one thing, retail vacation agents don't have as many definite requests for products as corporate agents do. They rarely hear, for example, "Get me a ticket to Houston, Wednesday, leaving here at 9:00 A.M." A vacation counsellor's work usually inivolves a great deal more research than such a simple request would entail. All in one day a vacation agent might have to find a two-week tour to Australia that includes the Great Barrier Reef, Ayers Rock, *and* a day on a sheep farm; hunt and peck for a tour to the mines in Kiruna, Sweden; and try to locate a company that handles adventure tours in Alaska.

In addition to doing research, the vacation agent may have to solve complicated, unforeseen predicaments: Clients may be touring a country when that government is overthrown and riots have become widespread. Another client may be stranded in a foreign land because the tour company suddenly has gone bankrupt. In the midst of this hectic day a person casually strolls into the agency and wants to chat about "going somewhere . . . this weekend."

Ayers Rock, Australia
Photo: Courtesy Australian Tourist Commission

So working in vacation travel is not always glamorous, easy, or fun. On the whole, though, it can be personally rewarding and financially profitable if the counsellor knows what he or she is supposed to do, how to do it well, and how to avoid causing problems.

VACATION (LEISURE) AGENT

Let's begin then by discussing what a vacation agent *does*. First of all, agents serve as a liaison between the suppliers and the buyers. They represent the travel suppliers to the traveler. Agents discuss and sell package tours and cruises each for one advertised price. And they can sell individual items such as hotel rooms, plane tickets, and car rentals.

After discussing package vacations or individual items the agent has to talk with the appropriate company (the supplier) who sells the item(s) and to book the reservation for the customer. The agent collects the customer's money, forwards it to the supplier, and receives and checks the tickets and vouchers (papers to be presented on the trip as proof of purchase of the trip).

VACATION COUNSELLOR

While not all agents are counsellors, all counsellors are also agents. (The exception is the counsellor who works as an independent and limits his or her service to dispensing travel information and advice to a client. Once counsellor and client have arrived at final decisions about the trip, the counsellor then turns the information over to an agent in a travel agency, who makes the reservations, prices the trip, collects money, and produces the necessary documentation.)

The functions of any counsellor are to evaluate, advise, recommend, guide, suggest, and prescribe. A counsellor also researches, creates, and arranges. And sells.

The vacation counsellor can be viewed as a traveler's investment broker. Customers meet with a travel expert to discuss how to spend their discretionary money. They want to find out where best their dollars can take them. They want to know about the selection of places and means of travel that are available for those dollars. A counsellor can influence vacation travel decisions about eight out of ten times.

COUNSELLING

Keep in mind that the goal of counselling is to sell. Often agents may become too enraptured with discussing exotic places and forget *why* they are doing so. This happens so often that many agencies have been reluctant to have their agents devote time to counselling. These agencies feel that the time spent is not profitable.

However, the result of the **counselling** is to **sell** travel products. And once again, the better a counsellor understands his or her duties and responsibilities, learns how to counsel with the intent of a sale, the more counselling time is reduced and sales closed.

There are certain personal strengths that *you* and every successful vacation counsellor need to handle your functions more smoothly and efficiently. You must draw heavily on your interactive people skills. And you must use your inner resources of imagination and creativity. You should draw heavily on all your knowledge of the world whether it's meteorology, archaeology, geography, history, psychology, or social studies. And you must practice your travel skills. You must utilize any and all material and people references and resources at your command.

REQUIRED PEOPLE ARTS

Perception—You don't need a degree in psychology to be classified as a good counsellor. But because you deal with your customer's emotions, dreams, and wants, develop the art of understanding and qualifying people. There are plenty of books available on the subject. Studying *Vacation CounSELLing* will improve your people arts through the art of communication.

Interpersonal Skills—These skills are necessary to establish rapport and gain your client's confidence. The client must trust you, respect your knowledge and judgment, and feel comfortable telling you about her or himself. You must connect with your customers, feel for them, and develop a solid working relationship. You want to hear the client say to you, "You know what I want."

Build this working relationship by:

1. *Listening* to what the client is saying. If you first listen to your client's ideas, impressions, and stories you will understand if the client knows what he or she has in mind and if it is being described properly. When you are listening to a client, focus on that person only. Stop any thoughts that may cause you to prejudge or drift away.

2. *Talking* with your client. Develop the art of questioning and making proper and timely remarks. Practice describing and talking in definite words of color, action, taste, smell, and touch, so the client can receive a clear image. Avoid "it's nice" and "it's a pretty place." Be more descriptive.

REQUIRED GENERAL SKILLS

Reading—Read about the past and what has survived in the world since prehistoric times. Read about the ancient Mayan culture and the ruins that remain. Read about travelers who have trekked the Annapurna Range in Nepal. Read the guidebooks, travel magazines, and trade magazines. You'll need to search through those guidebooks, journals, and brochures to find information about a country or place for your clients. You also need to read about current events. Know where the

World's Fair is this year. Know about the new cruise ships entering the waters this spring.

Writing—You'll write letters, day-by-day descriptive itineraries, and vouchers. You may possibly develop newsletters, brochures, and flyers. In scheduling a vacation, when the client gives you $7,000, you give pieces of paper (vouchers, letters) in exchange. In other words, for $7,000 the client doesn't receive the "real vacation," just papers that say it has been bought. Those papers aren't exchanged for the actual trip until the trip begins. So the words on those papers become very valuable to the traveler. Show the client that you regard this exchange highly. Use correct grammar and spelling. Type neatly.

REQUIRED KNOWLEDGE

Geography—The travel business, particularly vacation travel, is place-oriented. Your knowledge of the countries, cities, mountains, and beaches of the world is essential. Know where the current "hot spots" are. Know where people can lie on the black sand beaches and where they can snow ski in July. Know where they can view coral reefs from a submarine. Be familiar with the favorite honeymoon havens. Have information on the safety of traveling in Southeast Asia. Know about the prices in Mexico. Be able to list what to see and do in London for a week.

You don't necessarily need to know how high the mountain is, but where it is, how to get there, and why people want to go there. This type of geography is called "destination geography." You may also hear it called "tourism geography."

Supplier Contacts and Reference Materials—Your network for gathering information is those persons and companies that provide your client with travel products such as hotel rooms, car rentals, tours, cruises, and airline seats. These suppliers promote their products in their brochures and in agent manuals. It is very important to know *who* these suppliers are and how good they are. They should be able to answer your questions about a hotel they sell, about a particular local market, about the sights in the area they sell. Continually increase your knowledge by drawing from their knowledge.

BENEFICIAL CHARACTER TRAITS

Helpfulness—Be willing to research and find anything. Check whatever needs checking. If clients want to know if they get a choice of entree from the dinner menu or if it's a set menu when they buy the hotel package, ask the appropriate source for an answer.

Accuracy—Have the desire to be right. Never assume. Check details. When travelers fly long distances they may want to know how long they'll actually be on the plane. Calculate the elapsed time; don't respond with a glib "quite a few hours."

Insight/Intuition—Listen to your gut feelings and reactions. If you "have the feeling" that the reservationist did not understand your request even though she took your information, call back and discuss it further. If you expected your client's documents in the mail by today and they are not here, do not give in to the easy answer that they must delayed in the mail. Call the company and check on them.

Foresight—Look beyond the immediate. What else do these people need? Often travelers don't know. Let's say your clients have booked flights from Seattle to Tokyo to Bangkok and the flights don't connect. They are forced into an involuntary layover in Tokyo. Immediately find out if the airline pays for the hotel, transfer, and meals during the stay. Ask the airline what the procedure is. Don't give your clients time to wonder about it. Have the answer before they ask the question.

Responsibility—You have the influence to make selections for travelers, but remember that you are accountable for your decisions, recommendations, and opinions.

PERSONAL QUALITIES

Keep the following qualities in mind as you build your success in vacation counselling.

1. *Be pleasant.* Smile when working.

2. *Be committed.* Vacation counselling cannot be done with half a heart. Your clients will know when you don't care. And, then, they will not use you.

3. *Accept challenge.* Whether your people want you to plan their trip to Bhutan or you've been asked to make a thirty-minute presentation to a group of fifty people, do it. Don't pass it off to "someone in the office more qualified." They asked *you.* It's time to become qualified.

4. *Accept change.* The only thing constant in travel is change. Air fares change. Names of countries change! The quality of hotels changes. People change their minds. You've just completed a sale to Paris for a week. Tomorrow these same people say they've decided not to go to Paris; they want to talk to you about a trip to Tahiti instead! Just cancel the Paris trip, and prepare a new trip—this time to Tahiti. No problem.

5. *Stay current.* Keep abreast of national and international affairs. You need to integrate the politics, weather, and health and safety situations of the destination into the itineraries and schedules. Keep abreast of trade changes and with the airlines and tour companies. Be aware of such dilemmas as ground transportation strikes.

6. *Believe in your abilities.* You, not your client, are in the travel business. You are the expert. You have all the resources and references at your fingertips. Let your clients know that you *can* help them.

7. *Use your resources.* Counselling demands resourcefulness. Think of alternatives. Think of special twists you can include in an itinerary.

8. *Be a communicator.* Listen. Talk. Listen.

9. *Be project-oriented.* A project is an organized undertaking achieved step-by-step over a period of time. The client comes into your office today to plan a three-

week rail trip through Western Europe departing six months from now. You will work on this trip piecemeal, a well as many others, during this six-month period.

10. *Look and act mature.* Vacation clients appreciate counsellors who look and act mature. Wear neat, coordinated business attire. For men this means coat and tie. For women, it means the skirted suit, a dress, or a blouse and skirt. Use correct grammar. No childish remarks. Control your gestures. Do not let personal phone calls and distractions interrupt your business transactions.

TRAVELING AS A TRAVEL COUNSELLOR

Before you began studying or working in the travel business, you most likely had the innate desire to travel yourself. And, possibly, you have already done some traveling. Now your work and your traveling become intertwined. You will have the opportunity to participate in travel agents' trips called *familiarization trips* (*fam* for short). Fam trips are sponsored by any airline, tourist board, hotel, cruise line, or tour company—worldwide, singly, or jointly. These suppliers use the fam as a form of direct advertising for their country or their products. They are your hosts and escorts. They have planned the itinerary, the meals, the events. They want you to sample, inspect, and evaluate what they have to offer. They hope that your participation in the trip will entice you to sell the places more actively and enthusiastically to your clients.

Invitations are distributed by suppliers to agency personnel. Some of the trips are free and some bear a fee. The cost, though, is minimal compared to the price that the traveling public would pay for such a trip. Sometimes the agent and sometimes the agency pays this fee.

Regardless of the fee and who pays it, a fam is a business trip, not a personal vacation even if you choose to go on a fam during your vacation time. You travel as a member of a group of travel professionals. You are required to attend all functions. If you are supposed to visit Varig Airlines' reservations center in Rio de Janeiro between noon and 2:00 P.M., that is where you will be, not at the beach or in the marketplace. Show enthusiasm. Be on time for all events; maintain proper decorum. You are a guest. Be courteous. Be interested in all that is provided for you. Refrain from making demands just because you are "in travel."

Dress neatly even if it's a beach fam. Dress appropriately. For instance, no jeans attire unless that is proper for an area such as Arizona or Wyoming.

By the way, there are two other travel privileges that come with your responsibilities. First, you are entitled to *airline passes* worldwide. Distribution of the passes, though, is at the discretion of the airline and your agency.

Second, you may also receive *personal discounts* from any supplier to be used during your free time or vacation. If you want to go on a cruise, for instance, contact the cruise line personally and establish what the discount will be.

But remember, when using all forms of travel and any type of discount, you are representing the travel industry. Yes, you will have fun, but always let your professional attitude and demeanor be evident.

REVIEW

SET 1

1. What is retail travel?

_____

2. Name three things a counsellor does.

_____

_____

_____

3. What is the goal of travel counselling?

_____

4. What is a fam trip?

_____

_____

_____

SET 2

1. How does a travel counsellor act as an investment broker?

_____

_____

_____

2. What can you do to increase your knowledge as a travel counsellor?

_____

_____

_____

3. What does it mean to be project-oriented?

_____

_____

_____

4. Why is it important that your written communications to clients be neat and presented well?

_____

_____

_____

_____

_____

_____

SET 3

1. You are a counsellor in an agency where everyone does everything. A client comes to you with a brochure advertising a tour that sounds interesting. Do you turn the person over to an *agent,* or do you deal with the client yourself? Why?

_____

_____

_____

_____

2. How *does* one act and look mature?

_____

_____

3. Name the personal qualities that counsellors should strive to attain.

_____	_____
_____	_____
_____	_____
_____	_____
_____	_____

2

UNDERSTANDING VACATION TRAVELERS AS A GROUP

KEY TERM
Market

We've just got to get away! It doesn't matter what shape the economy is in. We may reduce our trip to seven days, but we will go.

Consumers travel on vacation for many reasons. Their three main objectives are: to recharge themselves mentally, physically, and emotionally; to learn or experience something out of their ordinary arena; and to have something they can relive for as long as possible through conversation.

There are as many kinds of trips that accomplish those objectives as there are people who want to go on them. They include city sightseeing trips, cruises, adventure trips, tours, spa/ranch/camp/resort stays, and sightseeing train rides. The type of trip that a traveler chooses depends on many factors. A traveler's age *may* play a part in the choice, but do not prejudge the type of trip a customer should go on by age alone. Don't *assume* that when customers in their fifties say they want to see Europe, they mean via escorted motorcoach tour; or when a customer is twenty-three or so that it will be by riding the rails. In determining the right trip for the client consider the client's lifestyle, attitude, intent, finances, ability, and the point at which he or she is in life.

KNOWING PEOPLE MARKETS

A people market categorizes general lifestyles and attitudes toward travel. It isn't indicative of an age, though people in certain age groups do gravitate toward certain places and activities. For example, a male in his twenties is more likely to enjoy riding motorcycles than a man in his sixties. However, this does not preclude a *particular* man in his sixties from riding a motorcycle. Also, any one person may fall into two or more markets. The sixty-year-old man is a mature citizen, but he is still physically fit enough to enjoy adventure trips.

Market information is helpful in determining trips. But remember that when dealing with any market, it is important not to stereotype. Deal with the customer as an individual. This chapter presents only general guidelines and overall tips for selling to various typical people markets.

The Mature Market is loosely categorized as that group over fifty-five years of age. Those from this market who visit you have time and money to travel. Do not assume that they will take a lot of your time with little financial return. True, many mature citizens are on a fixed income, but a large part of their income goes to discretionary items. In fact, Americans over fifty earn more than *half* the discretionary income in the country. The median income of couples sixty-five and over in 1986 was $28,375, which can go a long way when mortgages are paid, the children are gone, and few large purchases are necessary.

Mature travelers not only have spending money, they are healthy enough to enjoy it. While there may be certain limitations due to overall aging in people over seventy-five, fully half of all people now seventy-five to eighty-four are free of health problems that require special care or that curb their activities. And in the over eighty-five group more than one-third report no limitation due to health.

Consequently, they participate in a wide spectrum of tours, ranging from domestic or international itineraries to exotic destinations; from short to long; from sedentary to active. The places most visited are Canada, Hawaii, Mexico, the Caribbean Islands, Western Europe, United Kingdom, and Asia/Orient. And *Modern Maturity Magazine*'s 1986 survey of its readership showed that 34.5 percent of the respondents take two or more trips a year.

The Upscale Market is that group of people who are affluent. Upscale travelers fall into two categories. Both engage in expensive trips. But one group prefers the utmost in luxury and quality and seeks magnificence and privilege. They fly first class, use chauffeur-driven limousines, and stay in suites in the world's finest hotels. If these travelers join a group, they elect to use a deluxe tour company that tailors the tour with plenty of options, limits the size of the group, and indulges its passengers.

The other group often seeks the unique and exotic. They may want to join a street dance in Lomé, Togo; pick up centuries-old pottery shards in Mongolia's Gobi Desert; or wander through the lunar landscape of Turkey's Cappadocia. They have the money to travel in pampered style, but they are willing to spend exorbitant amounts for expensive, uncomfortable trips as long as the destination has not yet

Ancient Cappadocia, Turkey
Photo: Courtesy Turkey, Office of the Culture and Information Attaché

been tapped by the average traveler or backpacker. People in this upscale market will spend $300 a day to share a room with flying and crawling roommates! Often, the rougher the trip, the higher the cost for the travel because it's in remote parts of the world. In these areas they will join an escorted tour operator, since using experienced guides is often the safest and smartest way to explore some of these places.

These upscale markets have something (in addition to money) in common; they both follow their dreams, whether it's standing breathless at the summit of snow-capped Mt. Kilimanjaro on the equator or staying at the Hotel Roemerbad during West Germany's elegant Roemerbad Musiktage (festival of the world's finest chamber musicians and soloists).

The Yuppie Market consists of those people aged twenty-five to thirty-nine who are urban professionals with incomes of at least $30,000 as singles and $40,000 as marrieds. They have busy, active lifestyles. Physical fitness is important to them. They lean toward soft adventure trips, cruises, and inclusive resorts. They like to be with people their own age. They enjoy going where everyone else is going this year. They crave quality. It doesn't always matter if the prices are not the lowest. They'll pay a higher price to get what they want, when they want it.

The Adventure Market people are those who are attracted to trekking and sports holidays. Here you'll find your backpackers. Financially, they look for a combination of value and fun. These travelers seek opportunities for discovery and self-renewal, as described in this excerpt from a trekker's journal in Nepal: "I have been mesmerized by the Buddhist stupas and Hindu temples, struck by the loveliness of the local people, and fascinated by observing life lived in its most elemental, desperately hard form. So much of the world we have glimpsed on this trip is so diametrically opposed to the style of life we knew before, that it causes the mind and the senses to reel. Values have to be adjusted, all prior input opened up and reassembled. New perspective has been gained which shall unquestionably remain with us forever. . . ."

These people value their individuality and independence. If they travel in a group, it's a small group of people who share their own interests.

The Bargain Market people more often equate the word "bargain" with "value" than with "cheap." While an advertised low price will get customers in this group in the door, they will buy only if that price represents a truly good deal. They are not poor people. They have money; they just don't want to spend it, at least not all on one trip, or frivolously. Their definition of a bargain is getting what they want at the lowest price possible.

You can book these people inexpensively, yet still give them the value they want by encouraging them to travel in the off-season (times when prices are drastically reduced because of lack of traffic). For example, summer in the Caribbean is off-season because it's hot; therefore, prices are greatly reduced. So if travelers go May 1, the beginning of the off-season, or later, instead of April 20 they can get the same hotel and amenities but for thirty percent less.

The Family Market consists of families who need vacations that provide something for everyone, such as national parks, theme parks, and cruises. They generally want discounts for the children, adjoining rooms, and children's menus. They look for cruise lines that have babysitters, and Club Meds that offer Mini-Clubs for children.

The Honeymoon Market generally wants a warm-weather destination with beautiful scenery. Over half of these newlyweds choose foreign destinations. Hawaii, the Virgin Islands, Bahamas, Bermuda, Mexico, and Jamaica are the top choices. Canada and Western Europe are also popular in the summer.

Regardless of the area, they prefer a romantic hotel, with good restaurants and white-glove service. They want a good room in the hotel. And they want to be left alone.

Younger newlyweds usually like to pay for as much of the cost of the trip as possible prior to departure because often they aren't experienced travelers and do not want to be embarrassed by financial shortcomings. These couples want to work with knowledgeable, attentive travel counsellors who can advise them on the choices and help them make financial decisions.

FANTASIZING ABOUT VACATIONS

Whether a person is a honeymooner or a mature citizen, knowing what a client's vacation fantasies are helps you as a counsellor, especially when all you know initially is a vague, "I want to go somewhere." Let's take a look at a survey of the American traveler, conducted by mail to four thousand households, to find out some of these fantasies. The study was done by the advertising agency D'Arcy Masius Benton Bowles Inc. The study asked consumers to choose from a list of thirteen fantasy activities. Here are the results:

MEN

1. Go on an African safari
2. Visit Mainland China
3. Camp in the wilderness
4. Fly in a hot-air balloon
5. Go white-water rafting
6. Gamble in Monte Carlo
7. Go on a manned space flight
8. Dine at the White House
9. Attend a Cannes film festival
10. Have a sexual encounter with a stranger

WOMEN

1. Gamble in Monte Carlo
2. Dine at the White House
3. Visit Mainland China
4. Fly in a hot-air balloon
5. Attend a Cannes film festival
6. Go on an African safari
7. Camp in the wilderness
8. Appear on a television talk show
9. Go white-water rafting
10. Go on a manned space flight

You can use this fantasy information to begin a conversation, or to get a customer's attention focused. Let's say the customer says, "I want to go someplace different because I'm bored," and that's all. To make this uncommunicative customer more enthusiastic and more quickly involved in the discussion, you can say, "How about going on safari in Africa?" You are not immediately recommending a product. You are simply getting the person interested. Realistically, the vacation may end up being the Molokai Safari Ranch in Hawaii or Busch Gardens in Tampa, Florida. Just because some clients tell you what their fantasies are or just because you suggest one doesn't mean they'll plunk the money down on the table to do it. But you may lead them to a similar activity that is not as far away, or one that can be more realistically achieved.

ISSUES AFFECTING VACATION CHOICES

Another survey that may help you in determining the best trip for your client is a recent study by *Better Homes & Gardens* about the issue of greatest concern to prospective travelers.

	Very important	Somewhat important	Not too important	Not at all important
Cost	67.9	24.8	3.5	—
Opportunity to relax and unwind	67.5	20.8	4.2	—
Interesting sights	67.5	23.7	1.8	1.1
Safety, concern for terrorism	61.9	15.3	7.7	16.0
Opportunity to explore; adventure	43.4	33.2	10.2	3.5
Good food	31.4	44.2	11.3	3.5
Activities/facilities for children	28.8	16.8	5.5	33.4
Availability of discounts or special deals	23.7	34.1	24.8	8.6
Good shopping	15.0	32.1	29.4	12.2

This information should help you put these matters in proper perspective when counselling. Note that the first four items—cost, opportunity to relax and unwind, interesting sights, and safety and concern for terrorism—rank high and are therefore not to be overlooked when dealing with anyone. But what constitutes relaxation, interest, concern, and cost is not the same to everyone. An upscale traveler may find the Venice Simplon Orient Express train ride relaxing and the scenery along its route interesting, while the adventure traveler would find riding a regular train second class with the local people more relaxing. And they may find these locals more interesting than the scenery.

Group and market guidelines do help, but remember to deal with the individuals within the group or market or survey. Find out what *their* feelings are. That sells leisure/vacation travel.

Trajan Forum, Rome
Photo: Courtesy Italian Government Travel Office

REVIEW

SET 1

1. What is a people market?

_____

_____

2. What two groups comprise the upscale market?

_____

_____

3. What are the top destinations for honeymooners?

_____

_____

_____

_____

4. Who comprises the mature market?

_____

SET 2

1. What yuppie traits are good to know in order to deal properly with people in this category?

_____

_____

2. What are most people really looking for when they want a bargain?

_____

3. Why do young newlyweds especially depend on a vacation counsellor to help plan the honeymoon?

_____

_____

_____

_____

_____

_____

SET 3

1. Why do people go on vacation?

_____

_____

_____

_____

2. What is wrong with stereotyping customers?

_____

_____

_____

_____

3. When counselling people about their vacations, how can you use a knowledge of their vacation fantasies?

_____

_____

_____

_____

3

UNDERSTANDING VACATION TRAVEL MECHANICS

KEY TERMS

Operator/Tour Operator

Wholesaler

Supplier

Commission

Professional Fees

Consortium

Preferred Supplier/Vendor

Vacation travel requires a network of people and resources to work out an itinerary and complete a trip. The network begins when a customer comes to the agent with a travel request. The agent, in turn, calls upon as many travel suppliers as are necessary to put together the trip the customer wants. The agent may, for example, request a seat on an airline, space in a hotel, and a reservation on a motorcoach tour. The individual travel suppliers then confirm these requests and send the necessary documents—airline tickets, vouchers, coupons, and the like—to the agent. When all the documents are in hand, the agent then gives them as a package to the client. The client embarks on vacation and presents the various documents as necessary to the individual suppliers, who provide the customer with all the components the agent has arranged—air transportation, lodging, sightseeing, meals, car rentals, rail tickets, whatever.

THE AGENT/CUSTOMER/SUPPLIER INTERDEPENDENCY

THE CUSTOMER'S CONNECTION TO THE TRAVEL AGENT/COUNSELLOR

As shown in chapter 2, the relationship between the agent/counsellor and the customer consists of the counsellor discussing and advising the customer on available vacation choices. The choices may be just a hotel in Las Vegas, or a cruise in the Caribbean, or an individualized day-by-day tour through France.

THE AGENT'S CONNECTION TO THE TRAVEL SUPPLIERS

Whatever the choice, the agent makes all the necessary arrangements with the various travel suppliers on behalf of the client. The agent may do this by booking each item separately or, if the customer has selected a "package" trip, the agent will contact the respective wholesaler or tour operator, who has already arranged the various items and is offering them as a package sold at one advertised price. *Tour wholesalers* and *tour operators* are also called *tour companies*. You will often hear all these terms used interchangeably, although there are some fine differences which are discussed below.

Las Vegas Strip
Photo: Courtesy Las Vegas News Bureau

Wholesalers and operators negotiate with individual suppliers for quantity pricing. They may buy round-trip airline tickets to London, bus transfers between the airport and the city of London, seven nights at the Savoy Hotel, and a Britain-shrinker day tour from London to Stonehenge. They then add up the individual costs, tack on a profit, and establish one set price for the total package. They design and print a brochure on this package, and distribute the brochure to travel agents and sometimes directly to the public.

One of the *differences* between wholesaler and operator is their relationship to the consumer. Operators often sell *directly* to the public as well as through travel agents. Wholesalers generally work *only* through travel agents.

THE CUSTOMER'S NEXT CONNECTION TO THE TRAVEL AGENT

The customer then receives all vouchers (evidence of payment) and tour documents (details of the trip) for the vacation from the agent, who has received them from the suppliers and operators.

THE CUSTOMER'S CONNECTION TO THE TRAVEL SUPPLIERS

It must be emphasized that the agent does not deliver the various products. It is the suppliers and the tour operators who deliver what was promised in the brochure. At various stages during the trip the customer presents tickets, vouchers, and documents as proof of purchase for the products.

For example, when the traveler arrives at the hotel, the voucher is presented in exchange for the room. When the traveler boards the tour bus, the document that states this is a paid member on the tour is presented. At this point the tour operator/supplier sees to the customer's needs and wants during the trip.

Another difference between a wholesaler and an operator is in the delivery of the actual products. The wholesaler *does not* operate any aspect of the tour; the suppliers do that. The tour operator, on the other hand, *may* operate some of the ground features, such as buses and the company's own tour escorts or guides.

HOW TO KNOW YOUR SUPPLIERS/OPERATORS

As an agent, you turn your customer over to the operators and depend on those companies to provide a good trip. It is absolutely essential, therefore, to select operators carefully.

Experience tells you which ones are good, reputable, and dependable. But it takes time to gain this experience. Below are other methods for careful selection.

- Attend trade shows in which hundreds of suppliers and tour companies participate. Meet their representatives; listen to them speak about their products and their companies.

- Talk to other agents and counsellors at these shows and anywhere else you can mingle with your colleagues. Ask them what experiences they have had with certain operators.

- Read trade magazines. There are two that regularly discuss the status of vacation operators: *Travel Weekly* and *Tour and Travel News.*

- Ask for client feedback. Your clients' remarks will help guide you in using the operator for future bookings.

- Go on familiarization trips sponsored and operated by the very suppliers and companies that you are considering for your clients' trips. What better way to know about suppliers than to have sampled their products yourself!

- If you are wary of an operator, consider calling ASTA's Ethics Committee or your state's travel organization. Check if any bad claims have been issued.

In order to feel more secure that what is promised to customers will be delivered, some travel agencies now package, sell, and escort their own tours. They go directly to the suppliers and negotiate their own rates for airline seats, hotel rooms, bus transfers, and sightseeing tours. After establishing one inclusive price, the agency then designs and prints its own brochure, promotes the tour through advertisements, sells the seats on the tour, and escorts the people who bought the trip from the agency. In this case, the agency acts as its own tour operator.

EARNING COMMISSIONS

When selling retail travel (single and packaged vacation products to individuals), the gross cost for a trip that is quoted to a customer equals the *net cost* that the agent owes the supplier or operator *plus* the *agent's commission* from the supplier for the sale. For example, the advertised gross cost of the seven-night London package is $800. Basic commission to an agent is ten percent, so the agent keeps $80 and sends the net cost of $720 to the operator. Commissions paid in this manner do not affect the cost of the trip to the customer. Even if the customer purchased the trip directly from the operator, the gross cost would be the same $800. The operator simply keeps the $80.

OTHER WAYS TO EARN MONEY

Some agencies and counsellors also charge for time they spend *discussing* travel arrangements. The payment that a client makes directly to the counsellor or agency for the advice, information, and recommendations is called a *professional fee.* Fees can be charged by the hour, destination, trip, or as a flat fee. It is in no way connected with the commission earned from operators.

Many agencies have also joined a *consortium*, which is a stock corporation. Here the travel agencies have banded together to implement stronger marketing strategies and to increase buying power. Collectively, they seek override (extra income above the basic ten percent) commissions from *preferred suppliers*. These suppliers have agreed to pay the consortium agents more money for sending them more business than they would otherwise. The agency tends to sell those suppliers who reward them the most.

It is up to the agencies to decide what to do with override payments. They are free to pass all or part of the money on to the traveler as a rebate, and, in fact, this is becoming more and more common as agents are using the rebate as an enticement to close a sale.

When an agency acts as its own tour operator, it controls the cost of the trip and therefore regulates the amount of commission it wants to earn. The agency as operator can tack on any amount to the net cost—obviously the resulting gross cost must be attractive to the buying public.

Eiffel Tower, Paris
Photo: Courtesy Air France

REVIEW

SET 1

1. Who or what are your travel suppliers?

_____

_____

_____

2. What is a professional fee?

_____

_____

3. Clients tell you that they want hotel reservations for seven nights in London and a full size car. You

_____ a. give them the phone number for the hotel so they can make the reservation

_____ b. tell them they'll have to get the car when they arrive

_____ c. contact the hotel and the car rental company and make the reservations for the clients

_____ d. type out vouchers with the requests and give the vouchers to the clients

4. When selling retail travel you quote clients

_____ a. gross cost

_____ b. net cost

_____ c. net plus commission

_____ d. anything you think they're willing to pay

SET 2

1. What are the differences between a tour operator and a tour wholesaler?

   Operator: _____

   _____

   Wholesaler: _____

   _____

2. What is the difference between commissions and professional fees?

   Commissions: _____

   _____

   Professional fees: _____

   _____

3. Why use preferred suppliers?

   _____

   _____

   _____

SET 3

1. Explain the cycle of transactions from the time a customer requests travel services and products to the time the products are used.

   _____

   _____

   _____

   _____

---

2. Discuss how agencies earn more commissions as a member of a consortium, and how your agency's membership affects your choice of products to sell.

4

MEETING THE CLIENT

KEY TERMS
Territory
Shopper
Rapport

Meeting the customer is the first step in a successful sales approach, and in many ways it is the most important. All the steps that follow—getting to know the customer, matching the client with a product, overcoming objections, and closing the sale—are in jeopardy if you mishandle this first step. It is very important to remember, then, that presenting yourself and your service comes before demonstrating and selling any products.

As we discuss meeting the client in this chapter, many of the points we cover may seem very basic or obvious to you. In fact, many of them are. But we are covering them here because, despite their obviousness, they are often overlooked and result in the loss of sales.

Let's start, then, by discussing this first step in the sales procedure—meeting the client. There are only two ways in which you greet a customer—on the telephone or in person. Either way, you create a first impression for that customer. And you don't get a second chance to make that first impression.Oftentimes, clients judge from the initial greeting whether they *want* to do business with the travel company or not. From the first instant of contact, therefore, focus on the person who is on the phone or who just walked in. Individualize each customer. This is when you begin to present yourself and to offer service.

GREETING THE CLIENT ON THE TELEPHONE

When dealing with a customer on the phone, the phone acts as your desk, the only physical item separating the two of you. When you reach for the phone, imagine yourself reaching for the client's hand, as you would if you were meeting in person.

As you reach for the client on the other end of the phone, smile, just as you would if the person were actually there. Now you are ready to speak. Over the phone, you only have two sales aids to use: *words* and *tone of voice*. How you employ these aids instinctively lets clients know whether or not they are valued as potential customers.

WORDS

The preferred opening line is the name of your travel company, then "this is" and your first name.

> Counsellor: "Magical Travel. This is [pause] Terry."

This format lets the caller know immediately that this is the right number and a real person is talking. Use your first name because the travel industry is a first name business; you want the caller to be comfortable with you. Similarly, if the customer identifies herself as "Jane Smith," call her Jane, unless you can tell that she is elderly. In this case, address her as Ms. Smith until and if she asks you to call her by her first name. If the caller identifies herself as Ms. Jones, she wants to be addressed that way.

> Counsellor: "Good morning. Magical Travel. This is Terry. How may I help you today?"

The preceding opener is too long. Also, it seems to indicate that Terry is the right person for the caller to be talking with. In fact, Terry may specialize in European travel and the caller may want information on Peru.

Don't allow this caller to get halfway through an investigation of the best route to Peru before discovering that this is the wrong person to speak to. Immediately interrupt and tell the customer that you will transfer the call to the right person. No one cares to repeat a question. And having to do so makes a potential customer skeptical of the efficiency of your company.

TONE OF VOICE

How should you sound when you greet a customer? *Definite* and *enthusiastic* and *focused*. Let the caller know that you are concentrating on the call, and not on your lunch.

Take your time with the opening line. Pause slightly before you speak your name so the caller is alerted to listen for it. Be aware of how you sound. Avoid sounding flat or dropping your voice. Also avoid speaking excessively slowly which may be interpreted as boredom, depression, or hesitancy. And speaking very quickly may give the impression that you're too busy or rushed. A sharp, loud pitch may be interpreted as anger with the company or with its clients. A choppy tone that alternates between high/low and fast/slow is often perceived as a lack of concentration on your part or an indication that you are distracted.

A sweet, young, high-pitched voice is generally unsettling to vacation travelers. Clients want to deal with mature counsellors. They want you to have had enough life experiences to help them plan their experiences. They want to feel that you're skilled enough to act as a financial advisor concerning their travel investments, and that you can make decisions and judgments for yourself and others. Controlling your voice is one of the ways to build this mature image. And you *can* control your voice. All it takes is awareness and a little practice. If you have a sweet, young voice, counter the impression that you are too young by modulating your voice. Take the youthful edge off of it. If you can't do this successfully, you run the risk of losing clients before you can demonstrate either your knowledge or your abilities.

ON HOLD

You've given your opening statement. The caller responds by asking for John. John is on another phone line, however. How should you answer this request to speak to him?

> Counsellor or Receptionist: "John is on another line. Would you like to hold, or may I take a message for him?"

Give the caller only two choices. More than that causes confusion. If the client wishes to hold, respond before you simply click off!

> Counsellor: "Thank you." *Or,* "Thanks, I'll tell him you're waiting."

The average time any of us can be on hold before we fidget or become irritated is seventeen *seconds*. So report back to the caller within that time period so that the caller can decide whether or not to hold for John.

> Counsellor: "Thanks for waiting. John is on another line. Would you like to continue to hold, or may I take a message for you?"

The reply, "thanks for waiting," is preferable to "I'm sorry you had to wait." Thanking callers makes them feel they've done the decent, professional thing. They commend themselves for being cooperative. They respond to you more, and in a tone that says everything is okay. On the other hand, when you say you're sorry, you arouse feelings of discontent. The caller may wonder what you're doing over there and what is taking so long. You need not be apologetic because your company has work to do.

CALLING CLIENTS

When you call a client, identify yourself in your opening statement.

> Counsellor: "Is Mary Johnson there? This is Terry from Magical Travel."
> *Or,* "This is Terry from Magical Travel. Is Mary Johnson there, please?"

When Mary comes to the phone and simply says hello, identify yourself again. Then give your reason for calling.

> Counsellor: "I have the answer about staying in the castle in England."
> "I have an alternate route for you."
> "I received your cruise documents today."

GREETING A CLIENT IN PERSON

A person who walks into a vacation travel company wants to be recognized and treated as someone important. So do just that. Recognize, individualize, and respect each client.

In person, you still create an impression with your choice of words and your tone of voice. But you can use your physical appearance, gestures, territory, and touch as additional sales aids.

PHYSICAL APPEARANCE

A travel agency or tour company is a business office. Business attire is suits, dresses, skirts, coats, and ties. If you look like you threw your wardrobe on in thirty seconds, if your shoe is untied, your necklace twisted around, and you forgot to put a belt on, clients may well be uneasy about your ability to keep their day-by-day itinerary in order. If your hair is flying off in all directions and the files on your desk are falling on the floor, they may wonder if you'll remember a detail such as getting them nonsmoking seats near the exit.

Look as if you want to succeed; package yourself to be orderly, organized, and "together." An international outfit of clanging bracelets from India, your *pareo* from Tahiti, and your wooden shoes from Holland tends to be viewed as conceit, not worldliness. (*Note:* If your company is doing an organized promotion to Grand Cayman, it's okay to dress up like a pirate to attract attention to the destination.)

GESTURES

Physical gestures (often called body language) are important at the moment of greeting as well as throughout the sale. In order for clients to want to do business with you, they must feel comfortable and secure. So greet them on their level when they walk in—stand up.

If you are working behind a counter, stand up but remain there. If you are working at an individual desk, walk around the desk and go toward the customer. Walk with purpose; walk as if it's important that you get there. Walk tall with your head up, shoulders back, stomach in. Look like a confident professional. The more confident you look, the more competent your clients view you.

Smile; focus on the client. Give your opening statement. The client knows this is Magical Travel, so you don't need to say so. You both know that help is wanted so don't ask, "Can I help you?" You are expected to help.

Instead, think of something to say that will begin the business transaction quickly.

>   Counsellor: "How may I help you today?"
>   "Where would you like to go today?"

The response will direct you to the next step. Suppose the client says, "I'm Rodney Forsyth and I'm here to talk to Kay about a trip to Hawaii."

Now, Kay has a private office. Guide this client where he needs to go. Don't leave him confused. Direct him through the office, just as a policeman would direct traffic through a busy intersection. Make the visitor comfortable and secure by motioning him to stop or to come on through.

Or tell him what to do. Say, "Just a moment, I'll tell Kay you're here." This signals him to stay where he is. Kay then tells you to escort him in. Don't yell at him across the room! Walk back to where he is standing. Give him a signal to proceed forward. Upon the client's entrance, Kay should stand up to greet him.

Now, let's say the client's opening line to you is, "I'd like some information about trips to Hawaii." Give an appropriate response, such as, "I'm glad you came in; we have lots of brochures. Have a seat at my desk." Give some directions, such as motioning to the appropriate chair. When the client sits down, you sit down.

TERRITORY

Americans like their space; don't invade it. As a general rule, remain about two and a half to three feet from the client. Usually keeping the desk between you establishes that distance. Stay on your side of the desk, even after you get to know each other better.

TOUCH

Americans also are uneasy about being touched. A handshake upon greeting and departing is very acceptable. But if you are inclined to touch the client at any other time, touch only an article of clothing. Touching the skin may be interpreted as an intimate or sexual gesture, and not appreciated. Or it may be considered an arrogant gesture on your part that you're now "old pals."

If repeat clients come in, give them the respect they're due. Familiarity is appreciated; intimacy is not. Don't take advantage of the familiarity. Stand up when you see someone you know. That gesture is usually enough for the client to walk to your desk automatically. Motion the person to have a seat, and sit down at the same time.

BURIED IN BROCHURES

A walk-in customer who immediately scurries to the brochure rack and hides nervously behind the folders is still due a courteous greeting. However, you may want to say "hello" as you are walking toward the person in order to call attention to yourself. Once you are within two and a half to three feet from, and squarely facing, the customer, make your opening remarks.

DO NOTS

The biggest mistakes you can make when greeting a client in person are

- Yelling at the client from your desk.
- Looking at the client but saying nothing.
- Making a one-word opening statement, such as, "Yes?"
- Looking at the client, then looking around the room, and hoping someone else has seen and will help this person.
- Not acknowledging a client's entrance/presence at all.

These bad manners are easy to fall into when you are very busy, not feeling well, or having other problems. A client should never be viewed as an interruption or a nuisance. Without clients you have no business. Without clients, you have no job.

ESTABLISHING RAPPORT AND CONFIDENCE

Rapport between you and your client needs to be established right away. Whether you first meet clients by phone or in person, you want them to determine immediately that they want to do business with you. A proper greeting is the first step toward establishing this rapport.

The more you focus on the client the more you build rapport. As you listen on the phone, make verbal responses, such as "mm, un-huh, ahh." Do not undertake other activities, such as straightening papers or gazing at the people outside the window while listening to the customer. Your tone of voice will reflect these distractions, and you will lose the rapport. Vacation clients are looking for a counsellor who cares about them and, at least for the moment, no one else.

Good words and phrases to use are

- I can. (I can have that brochure for you by Friday.)

- I'll ask. (I'll ask the tour company for a time schedule.)

- I understand. (I understand you hate hot weather so the best time to go will be April.)

- Personally. (I'll take care of that personally.)

- Today and Now. (Those are the fares today.)

When the client is in your office, you can strengthen the rapport even further by leaning toward and looking directly at the customer as you are listening. These gestures will also help you keep your focus where it should be—on the client. After listening to the client, begin your responses with words or phrases you just heard:

Client: "We haven't been to Hawaii before. Can you tell me something about the islands?"

Counsellor: "Though you haven't been there, have you read any books about the area or talked to others who have visited Hawaii?"

Client: "Well, we watch *Hawaii Five-O.*"

Counsellor: "What about the show attracts you to Hawaii?"

Client: "The beaches. We want beaches and surfing."

Counsellor: "Some of the best beaches and surfing are on the island of Oahu."

You have found out what the client is interested in by listening. Now the client will listen to you as you describe Oahu.

CONFIDENCE

Once the client is comfortable with you and has decided to do business with you, you must create the feeling that you *can do* the job. To gain the client's confidence, speak with authority. Avoid hemming and hawing. Phrases such as I can't (I can't get a seat for you until next week), I'm afraid (I'm afraid you can't leave until much later), and let's go over it to be sure I've got it right, all show a lack of confidence in your efforts and abilities. If you are confident you can do good things, clients will trust you with their dreams and money.

Jamaica
Photo: Courtesy Jamaica Tourist Board

SPOTTING A SHOPPER

Every person who comes into your office should be treated as a bona fide buyer. They may not buy right away. They may call or visit several times to gather information and to gain confidence in you as a competent agent. Be patient with these folks. They can become good, repeat customers. On the other hand, there are some people who will never buy from you. They simply like to visit your office with its colorful travel posters, look at the pictures in the brochures, and fantasize about visiting exotic locales. Worse, they love to chat with you and gather information about their fantasy trip. But they will never buy! All they will do is waste your time. These people are known in the trade as "shoppers" and it is important that you learn to distinguish between them and those cautious customers who are just slow to buy.

Here are some indicators that you are dealing with a shopper who is just wasting your time:

- Won't give you a name. When you ask with whom you're speaking, the response is, "Oh, I just wondered if you have any deals to Nassau."

- Plays travel agent. This person already has the answers, but continues to ask the questions. For instance, "I understand that the best time to go to Thailand is November. Right? Do you think it's safe to ride the bus into the mountains north of Bangkok? I don't think it is."

- Gets angry quickly. This person calls "just for information on group fares to Peru." But you are not in the group department so you refer the person to Sally. However, Sally is on another line at the moment. You say, "Will you hold for her?" And the response is, "Listen, all I want is an estimate. Can't you do that?"

- Shifts from one destination to another, unrelated one. "I'd like information on London and Alaska. I plan to go for one week in August."

- Gathers brochures, any brochures. "Could you send me brochures on the Caribbean Islands?" You begin asking questions so you'll know which brochures to send. There is reluctance to answer your questions. "I haven't got time now. Couldn't you just send some brochures?" (*Note:* If a person comes into the agency and asks for brochures, ask questions. If you don't seem to be getting many answers, just give out any brochure on the destination mentioned, along with your business card, and let that be the end of it.)

The majority of shoppers will not take the time to come in, however. They will call on the phone. How do you get rid of shoppers without being rude and without investing time or money in them?

For Person No Name, for the destination shifter, or for brochure gatherers, invite them in. Say that you have so much available that it will be necessary to come in and make a selection. If such callers are indeed shoppers, they won't come in. If the person *does* come by, then this may really be a buyer who has just been hesistant or looking for someone for some direction.

For the person who already knows the answers but continues to pester, respond, "You already have your information. Is there anything else I can do for you?" The response will probably be "No, thanks. I'll call you back." No call will come because you didn't play the game. (*Note:* Do not ask that question of a confirmed buyer. Someone who has bought something from you will buy more. For the buyer, be specific about what else you have available.)

REVIEW

SET 1

1. How long should you keep a customer on hold before getting back? _____

2. What is the acceptable physical distance between you and the customer during sales transactions? _____

3. What are some good words and phrases to use that express confidence?

   _____

   _____

   _____

4. A client walks into the agency. Should you
   _____ a. go to lunch
   _____ b. say, "Good grief! What do you want?"
   _____ c. drop your pen, and while you're picking it up, hope that someone else will see and help the customer
   _____ d. stand up, approach the client, and say, "What can I help you with today?"

5. When calling a client, the first thing you do is identify yourself. What's the second thing?

   _____

SET 2

1. Answer your phone at work. Have your travel classmates tell you how you sound. How *should* you sound?

   _____

   _____

   _____

2. Why does the phrase "thanks for waiting" get better results than "I'm sorry you had to wait"?

_____

_____

_____

_____

3. What impression of your travel work does the client get when you look like something the cat just dragged in?

_____

_____

_____

4. Name three behavior clues that tell you a telephone caller may be a shopper.

_____

_____

_____

SET 3

1. A client you know walks in and heads straight for your desk, peers down at you, and begins talking. What physical gestures should you use to make the situation more comfortable?

_____

_____

_____

2. You are in the office alone. You have a customer at your desk, and another phone rings. What do you do?

_____

_____

_____

_____

3. What is a good time to ask, "Is there anything else I can do for you?" When shouldn't you ask that question?

_____

_____

_____

_____

_____

_____

5

GETTING
TO KNOW
THE CLIENT

KEY TERMS
Direct Question
Indirect Question

If you have been successful in the first step in vacation sales—meeting the client—then you are now ready to proceed to the second—getting to know the client. Warning: This step is often overlooked or rushed through in order to sell a product quickly. You must devote time to get to know clients; otherwise, you run the risk of creating such problems as finding no product to satisfy them, losing contact with them before they buy, or being forced to handle complaints about a vacation that the clients feel was ill-suited for them. These problems are time-consuming and unprofitable. In order to be on the mark with your sale, get to know the client as a buyer, as a member of a group, and as an individual.

UNDERSTANDING HOW PEOPLE BUY

There are certain characteristics common to people who buy. Knowing these characteristics will help you when selling vacations. The eight most common characteristics are listed below along with a counselling situation to illustrate how to deal with each.

1. People like to buy; they don't like to be sold. They are suspicious of slick, fast-talking, exuberant salespeople. If the clients ask to see some packages on Hawaii and you immediately pull out *Go Hawaii*'s brochure and push it on them, it raises questions such as, what's your relationship with the tour company and what's your rush? Maybe *Go Hawaii* is a preferred supplier for you, but is it the right trip for these clients? Instead of making a product pitch, you should engage your clients in a give-and-take conversation to determine who is the best supplier for them.

2. People feel more secure in the present than in the future. Because the vacation is planned for the future, vacationers tend to put off the final decision. They worry if grandmother will be okay if they go. They wonder if the currency exchange will fluctuate too much by the time they get there. Counter this buying fear by using the words *today* and *now*. They know how grandmother feels today. They know what they can do now. Book them with a tour operator who guarantees today's quoted price!

3. People expect fast. Vacation clients expect fast answers from your computer on the price of their itinerary, Atlanta/Tokyo/Bangkok/Singapore/Hong Kong/Honolulu/Atlanta, just as they expect a quick answer from the bank on the amount of money in their account. They expect to know immediately what the differences are between first, second, and third class on the trains in Malaysia just as they expect a fast answer about the features of two different television sets. However, in vacation travel, "fast" is an expectation that often cannot be met. Sometimes you wait days for another person to get back to you with an answer, or to get through on the lines, or for Malaysia to return the telex (only to receive half an answer). Frustration is the result of unmet expectations. You can do three things to help prevent client frustration: One, do not promise fast unless you are absolutely sure it can be done fast. Two, allow more time to produce a result than *you* expect it will take. (If you or the supplier produces quicker results, your clients are impressed; if you take the expected time, your clients are satisfied.) Three, explain the time element to the clients so they will adjust their expectations.

4. People don't like to wait. People run on a schedule. When clients stop by your agency during their lunch hour they may be annoyed or disappointed if they have to wait to see you. Similarly, when they call you on the phone and you have to put them on hold, they begin to fidget after seventeen seconds. Counter this "wait" irritation by acknowledging their presence if they're in your office, or, if they're on the phone, by getting back to them every few seconds to tell them of your progress or just to let them know you haven't forgotten them.

5. People like personal service. Too often in our increasingly technocratic society people have been reduced to mere numbers. Do away with this numbers syndrome by giving them the personal service they deserve. Get their names and use their names. Let them know your name. Establish a rapport and a real relationship with them. They should be able to say to their friends, "Susan, *my* travel counsellor, . . ."

6. People need reassurance. Travelers can call an airline three different times with the same question and get three different answers. One result of this is that they aren't sure what to believe, and more than ever will shop for a travel agent until they get one who is confident and knowledgeable. A clue that they are reaching out for the security of accurate information is that they will repeat what you just said. "The plane leaves, then, at 2:15 P.M.?" Reassure these people by giving additional information or rephrasing what you've said. "Yes, that's right. It leaves at 2:15 P.M."

7. Many people don't read. Clients often only skim over the printed brochures and contracts. This results in errors and lawsuits. It is the travel agent/counsellor's responsibility to ensure that clients have a complete understanding of all terms and conditions regarding what they've purchased. Show them where the terms are written and what the brochure says concerning:

- What has been purchased; what's included
- Payment schedules
- Cancellation penalties
- Receipt of documentation

Hong Kong
Photo: Courtesy Hong Kong Tourist Authority

Even when you present clients with the final documents for a trip, review what is in this documentation packet. And when you give clients their airline tickets, recap what the itinerary says.

8. People don't like a *too-busy* attitude. People don't want to know that you're too busy. They are not impressed when you tell them how much work you have.

Do not say, "I'm sorry I haven't called you back sooner but the phones have been jumping off the hook," or, "Now where is your file; it's gotten buried underneath all this work," or, "I have been so busy, I haven't had time to work on your trip yet."

DEALING WITH DIFFERENT AGE GROUPS

Every age group has certain general similarities. Knowing what they are can help you serve them better. Following is a breakdown of various age groups and some of the traits common to those in each group. Always keep in mind, however, that any one individual in a group may not share those traits. Beware of stereotyping anyone, just because they are in a particular age group.

The *seventy-year-olds* and older remember the days when they knew their neighbor, the paperboy, and the man running the general store. They want to know you. They are more formal with introductions so call them Mr. or Mrs. or Miss. They also remember when people had time for one another. They want your time; don't look at your watch during the session. If you have an elderly client who is hard of hearing, talk with a strong, deep voice, and talk more slowly. Don't shout!

The *sixty-year-olds* remember the depression. They recall being without, so they usually plan ahead so they won't be without again. They don't care for surprises on their vacation. When it comes to traveling, they want information about everything that's included before they depart. They will spend noticeably more time with you discussing all the fine details; estimates and generalities are not enough for them.

The *fifty-year-olds* may also remember the depression and don't want to be without. But they tend to be more flexible on their trips. They like to be offered more choices (of hotels, locations, cruise ships) than do older groups.

The *forty-year-olds* like the vacation packages that offer gifts—hard-to-get theater tickets, two for the price of one, a first-time offer—which they tend to buy because it seems special. This group always seems ready for fun, and thinks less about consequences. They don't seem to deal as well with conflict as some younger groups.

The *thirty-year-olds* are the 1960s generation. They like fast; they'll like to watch you work your computer. When buying a vacation, usually they'll want to know what their rights arc and what the rules are, so be specific and cover these things thoroughly and they'll be happier. They understand that things can go wrong in the world, so they handle conflict well. That doesn't mean you should sell them a poor trip. It just means that they aren't as quick to place blame.

The *twenty-year-olds* are the *"Now"* generation and are a very independent lot. They usually want information from you, and then they'll do their own trip. Honeymooners in their twenties, though, do depend more on you to plan their trip.

Teens should be treated seriously; they, too, grow up. When they come into your agency they are usually gathering information for someone else—parents or grandparents. Be sure you give them your professional courtesy. Be sure to give them your business card to take home.

HOW TO ASK QUESTIONS

The way to know clients is to ask questions. The information you receive about them helps you determine how to deal with them. It determines which market, if any, they're in; which age group; how individualistic they are in their buying habits. The goal of questioning is to match the right product to the client.

Before you can ask a question, however, first *listen* to the client's request. Then *acknowledge* that you are listening by making listening responses. If the client is in your office, you can also nod your head. *Respond* to what you hear by repeating some of the words the client uses, or assessing what was said by rephrasing. At this point, *ask* for more information—ask a question. Then *listen* to the response.

There are two ways to ask a question: directly and indirectly. A direct question simply asks a question such as, "When do you plan to go? Would you like to book a return?" It should elicit a direct answer. However, if the client doesn't like to answer direct questions and is slow to reveal what is desired, switch to indirect questions. This is especially true if you don't know the client well. For example, if a person calls you requesting brochures on Cozumel, Mexico, and you ask, "When are you planning to go?" and the response is "I don't know yet," switch to an indirect statement: "Knowing when you're going will help me send you the right brochures." If you then get a better answer, you have a greater chance of continuing the conversation.

Another good time to use an indirect question is when you are following up with a prospect to see if the information was received. It will show your interest in the trip. For example, "This is Jan from Magical Travel. I'm interested in knowing what you thought about the vacation options to Alaska that I sent you."

Another technique to use when a client gives evasive answers is to select an answer yourself. For example, if the client expresses a desire to go on a trip "sometime in the summer," you can respond, "Let's look at hotel availability for July 15." If July 15 is good, you have successfully moved the conversation forward. If the date is not good, the client usually will be quick to say so and give you a more feasible date. "July 15 is a bit early. Check August 3." You still get the information you need.

Good phrases to use are:

- I'm interested
- I'd like to know
- I need to know
- I'm wondering
- Knowing _____ will _____

These openings reflect a concern, an involvement, a need, or want, and indicate that you have a real interest in the client and not just in making a sale.

QUALIFYING THE CLIENT'S TRIP

You need six basic pieces of information before you head in any sales direction. Get the *who, what, when, where, how,* and *why* of the trip. When a client simply asks for brochures to be mailed, get as many of these answers as you can so you know whether to send tour folders, hotel pamphlets, general information brochures, or a selection of these.

WHO

Who is going is not always clearly stated. Ask. Do not assume that the person requesting information is the one going. Do not assume that because the person says "I" that she's going alone. If you do assume, you could be selling this fifty-year-old woman a sedate escorted tour of Europe when it's her two wild, adventurous sons who are going. She is just doing the research and buying it for them.

WHEN

When they are going needs to be determined as early as possible in the conversation. If they want a warm place in December, that eliminates Bermuda as an option. If they want skiiing in July, that eliminates Colorado. Remember, when you have people who can't seem to tell you when, pick a date, any feasible date. If it isn't the date they want, they will be quick to correct you and give you the answer you need.

How long is also part of the "when" question. The answer helps determine not only price, but also if the "what" and "where" are feasible within the client's proposed time frame for the trip.

WHERE

You need specifics. Some clients start out with a general request like "Europe" or with the very general response of "somewhere." They usually do have *some* idea. They just don't know how to tell you, or they don't want to limit themselves until they hear what you have to say.

If the answer is "somewhere," follow up with qualifying questions such as, "warm or cold climate?," "near or far?," "a place close enough for a weekend, or farther away?"

If the answer to your question is still too general, for instance, "Germany," qualify further. Ask if they have been to Germany before; where in Germany have they been? Do they want to return to the same place or go to a new area?

WHAT

The type of trip needs to be determined, whether it's to be a busy sightseeing itinerary or a cultural/shopping expedition. For example, if they want a Caribbean vacation with plenty of tennis as a priority, you may book them into a tennis club or on a tennis package. But if all they want is plenty of sun and relaxation, you may select a small, quiet beach bungalow.

HOW

The details of the method of travel need to be discussed. The major *how* question is the mode of travel. Will it be by plane, train, boat, local buses, car rental, motorcoach, or a combination? Knowing how clients prefer to integrate the methods into the overall trip helps you make proper touring selections and prepare the itinerary. For instance, ask them:

- At what *pace* they want to travel.
- How much time they want at each event or place.
- How much leisure/free time/unplanned time they want.
- If traveling with a group, whether they prefer large (forty-two people) or small (fifteen to twenty-four) groups.
- If choosing the motorcoach tour, how important food is.
- If they like most meals taken care of, and if they want a choice of entrees or an a la carte plan.
- How important accommodations are in terms of quality, price, amenities, and location.

PROBING FOR THE WHY OF THE TRIP

The *why* of the trip is really two questions: one, what do they want to leave behind when going on vacation, and two, what do they expect to come home with (other than souvenirs and no money). Knowing the clients' answers to both will direct you to the right destinations and products for them.

A vacation should rejuvenate the body, mind, and spirit. At the basis of rejuvenation is change—of scenery, atmosphere, and/or activities. So ask your clients to think about what activity, atmosphere, or scenery they would like to be without for awhile or to change. Be aware that many people may not be accustomed to sharing their feelings with an agent. These are often the people who return from a trip and say, "It just wasn't what we were expecting," though they were not explicit with the agent beforehand about what they *did* expect. To throw some light on their reasons for the vacation ask them what they would like to leave behind: schedules, noise, caretaking, reporting to others, boredom, pollution, traffic, and/or decision-making. Invite them to tell you what change they need.

If you and the clients understand and verbalize the other *why* for the trip (what the clients expect to come home with) before selecting products, there's a good chance the clients will be happy with the outcome, whether it's sweet memories or whatever has been achieved, instead of being depressed about being home again and wondering why they even went. So ask them what they expect to achieve: an education, an adventure, self-discovery, the chance to meet and be with people or a rest away from people, excitement and fun, or quiet relaxation.

Let's say the clients are interested in an inclusive club in the Caribbean. If you know that they want to avoid schedules, back-to-back activities, and making decisions, and want to return home with the memory of time together, you might suggest Sandals in Jamaica (which is a more reserved inclusive club) rather than the Club Med in Martinique (which is action-packed).

SUMMARY: ASKING QUESTIONS

The who, what, when, where, how, and why can be asked in any order depending on how much information the client automatically volunteers. But get the answers early in the conversation. And get the answer to all these questions before you make any suggestions.

When the client says, "We'd like to go somewhere warm. Any suggestions?" you should not answer, "Yes, go to the Bahamas." Such a quick, direct response is wrong because you don't know these people yet. You don't know if they've been to the Bahamas ten times already. You don't know if they want to stay in the United States or travel out of the country. You don't know if the destination is feasible for the intended time of year. Qualify your customer by asking questions.

St. Barts, Caribbean
Photo: Courtesy French West Indies Tourist Board

USING A CLIENT VACATION REQUEST SHEET

You will have many sales conversations during a day. Keep them straight. Remember that the Antons want golf in Bermuda and the Rolands want tennis in the Bahamas, not the other way around. Keeping a formal record on each vacation request insures greater accuracy and it provides a guide to be sure you cover everything. And because it keeps information collected in one place, there is less likelihood of a scrap of paper with vital information getting stuck away in a book or falling off the desk into a wastebasket.

On the form include the following information:

```
NAMES _____

ADDRESS _____

PHONE NUMBER _____ NO. IN PARTY _____

CHILDREN (AGES) _____

SENIORS _____ HANDICAPPED _____

DATES AND TIMES _____

PREFERENCES IN LOCATION _____

MAIN OBJECTIVE FOR THE TRIP _____

ACTIVITIES TO BE INCLUDED ON THE TRIP _____

TYPES OF ACCOMMODATIONS PREFERRED _____

COST RANGE _____

LAST TRIP TAKEN (WHERE AND WHEN) _____

MOST MEMORABLE ITEM ABOUT THE TRIP _____

WHAT YOU WANT OUT OF YOUR VACATION _____

NOTES/COMMENTS _____
```

REVIEW

SET 1

1. In what two ways can you ask a client a question?

   _____

   _____

2. Why do you have to ask your clients questions?

   _____

   _____

3. What are the two parts of the *why* question you need to ask customers?

   _____

   _____

4. A new client arrives at your office. You greet her, and then she says, "I would like you to help me plan my vacation, but I don't know where I want to go." Which of the following is your most appropriate opening?

   _____ a. Suggest a cruise.

   _____ b. Ask her how much money she wants to spent.

   _____ c. Ask her when she wants to go on vacation.

   _____ d. Get her address and phone number.

5. List three reasons why you should fill out a vacation request sheet for each client's trip.

   _____

   _____

   _____

SET 2

1. Now that you know people expect fast, how can you counter it to be sure they are not irritated with the time factor involved when buying vacation products?

    _____

    _____

    _____

2. When selling travel you should be enthusiastic but not exuberant. Explain or demonstrate the difference.

    _____

    _____

3. How are clients apt to feel when you tell them how busy you are?

    _____

    _____

    _____

    _____

4. Should you use different sales manners when dealing with seventy-year-olds and thirty-year-olds?

    _____

    _____

    _____

    _____

    _____

    _____

    _____

SET 3

1. Mr. Brady comes into your office and says to you, "I'm planning another trip to the Orient. This time I need to stop in Hong Kong, Taipei, Tokyo, Bangkok, and Jakarta. How much will the air fare be?" What's your answer?

_____

_____

_____

_____

_____

2. "My husband and I would like to go somewhere warm the week of January 10 for about $1,000 a person. Any suggestions?" How do you propose to continue this common opener?

_____

_____

_____

_____

_____

3. Some people don't read. These clients want that cheap charter to Rio de Janeiro. There is a waiver they must sign. What can you do to make sure they know it's *their* responsibility to understand and abide by the terms and conditions of the tour before they sign?

_____

_____

_____

_____

_____

6

CONVERSING WITH THE CLIENT

KEY TERMS
Misrepresentation
Disclaimer
Seasoned Traveler

Before we go to step three in the sales procedure—matching the products to the client—we need to learn how to talk with the client so there are no misunderstandings about what we are selling.

Vacation counselling is a conversation for the purpose of selling travel. It is not a leisurely chat about how beautiful New Zealand is for its own sake. During the exchange of information you learn about your clients. But, remember, they view things from their frame of reference and you from yours. To guard against misinterpretation, misrepresentation, or information falling in the cracks between you, be careful how you say what you say.

TALKING THE CLIENT'S LANGUAGE

Your client is the traveler; you are the travel counsellor. The client talks like a traveler; and because you want to be understood without error, you should also talk like a traveler.

TRAVEL JARGON

Therefore, do not use travel industry jargon. Avoid *IT number, option date, elapsed time,* and *FCUs*. Such terms are of no value in the sale because they tend to confuse and intimidate the client. Instead, convert the terms into layman's language. Simply give the date when the deposit needs to be paid without using the words "option date." State how long the client will be on the plane, but don't refer to it as "elapsed time."

WORDS WITH MULTIPLE MEANINGS

Certain words and phrases are used regularly by both travel counsellors and travelers, but they may not mean the same thing to each group. The best way to avoid confusion is not to use these words and phrases at all. However, that may be difficult. So when you or the client uses them, follow up with a concrete fact, example, or description to clarify that you both mean the same thing. The most common words with different meanings are:

First class vs. deluxe. The traveling public often considers first class to be top of the line. For the industry it's the middle category. Deluxe is top of the line.

Oceanview vs. oceanfront. The traveling public thinks oceanview room means a direct view of the ocean from their window. To the industry an oceanview room means a peek at the water if you lean over the balcony! Oceanfront guarantees that you have a full view of the water right from your window or balcony.

Direct vs. nonstop. The traveling public thinks that flying direct means no stops between origin and destination. For the industry a direct flight is one that makes stop(s) en route but involves no change of planes. Nonstop means there are no stops.

Stop vs. stopover/stayover/delay/change of planes. Few terms are as confusing as these, partly because we in the industry often misuse them ourselves, and partly because the meaning of some of these terms can change depending upon circumstances. To the general public a stop may mean a stopover, a stayover, or a delay. To the industry, however, a stop means, or *should* mean, a touchdown of less than four hours domestic, of less than twelve hours between domestic and international, or less than twenty four hours international that *does not involve a change of planes.* A stopover is a touchdown of more than four hours (or more than twelve or twenty-four, depending) that may or may not involve a change of planes. Just don't make the basic mistake of using stop and change of planes interchangeably, and if you follow up any of these terms with a good description or example, you can avoid misunderstanding.

WORDS WITH RELATIVE MEANINGS

There are also common everyday words and phrases whose meanings must be viewed from the traveler's perspective and not from yours. Otherwise you'll erroneously sell your idea, not the clients'. And they'll find out too late that what they bought is not what they *thought* they bought. The words most misconstrued are:

Warm/cold

Nice

Small/big

Walking distance

Overlooking

Nearby

One person's idea of a nice beach may be seclusion and privacy. Your idea of a nice beach may be lots of interesting people and plenty of activities. If the word *nice* is tossed between you with no added description or discourse, you'll end up misleading the client to that *nice* (quiet?) beach at Acapulco.

To one client 80 degrees in Acapulco may be warm; to another it may be hot. It is wisest for you simply to say that the average temperature in Acapulco is 80 degrees. Let the individual client judge whether that's warm or hot or cold.

INDEFINITE WORDS AND PHRASES TO AVOID

Vague or indefinite terms can create uncertainty, and put doubt in the client's mind. If you say the client's ticket is *probably* being delivered, is it? If you say *maybe* the tour company has a safari trip that includes both Kenya and Tanzania, does it? If you say you *don't know* if the hotel renovations are completed, are they? If you're *afraid* it's still hurricane season in the Caribbean, is it? Speak positively, and if you don't know an answer, find out.

Another situation that suggests that you are not certain about your work or the facts is to propose to the client that you go over the arrangements "to be sure I've got it right." Such a statement jeopardizes confidence in you. If you are in need of clarification from the client, say, "Let's recap," and then summarize the transaction.

SENTENCES THAT SAY TOO MUCH

You will be giving clients a lot of important information. You need to make sure they hear all of it. Research shows, however, that we have short attention spans when listening to others. So speak in a way that your clients will hear you. Separate important pieces of information.

Counsellor: "You will need to get your passport renewed. After you get your passport back, [pause] you will need to get visas for Hungary and Poland."

If you say these two important things in one sentence, odds are that the clients will hear only the first item. Their attention span is over. It is as if you never told them about the second item. Consequently, errors and omissions occur. Problems arise.

> Counsellor: "You will need to get your passport renewed and you'll need to get visas for Hungary and Poland."

The clients will go ahead and get their passports renewed. But when you check to make sure they've done that *and* got the visas, they may say that you never told them they needed visas.

LEGAL LIABILITIES FOR WHAT YOU SAY/DON'T SAY

The travel agent faces potential liability situations every day. Difficulties may arise between the operator and the traveler that catch the agent in the middle even though the agent acted solely as a broker. In other situations the agent/counsellor may be directly liable for injuries or damages. This text does not purport to give legal advice, and recommends that any potentially litigious situation be discussed with an attorney. However, the following guidelines may prove useful in avoiding *misrepresentation, errors, omissions,* and *failure to disclose information/hazards.*

Misrepresentation. If you as an agent/counsellor volunteer information based on personal knowledge, and the information is deemed incorrect by the client, you can be held liable.

> Counsellor: "You will love this hotel; I've stayed there. It is so deluxe; service is impeccable."

The client takes the counsellor's word and stays at that hotel. The client considers the hotel to be an average place; actually, the service is lousy. The client says that your information was misleading; that you took money for it. The hotel was not what the client was told it would be.

How to avoid making unknowing false statements:

1. Do not sell *your* trip to *the client.*

2. Talk facts, not opinions. Or, if you talk opinions, say definitively to the client that it is someone's *opinion.*

3. Obtain a brochure on the hotel/tour/cruise so clients can see for themselves what the place looks like. It's then the operator/supplier who is representing the property or tour, not you.

4. Talk as the middleperson, which you are. Say, "Club Med has an inclusive resort in Paradise Island. Delta has the flights to the Bahamas in the mornings." Avoid, "*I* have an inclusive resort that is available, and *I* have flights available in the morning."

5. Always seek your client's approval. "How does it look to you? Is this what you had in mind?"

6. Put in your record, "Customer advised on this date that the hotel's swimming pool may not be open."

Errors. You make a mistake! You said a visa was not needed for Argentina, and it was.

How to avoid making mistakes:

1. Stay awake.

2. Realize that international affairs change constantly. Just because a visa was not needed six months ago doesn't mean it isn't now.

3. Always check your facts. Never assume. Never guess.

Omissions. You fail to tell a client something or fail to provide something that is necessary for the trip. For example, you failed to mention a recent outbreak of polio there, or you neglected to say that if the trip is cancelled the client won't get any money back.

How to avoid omission liability:

1. Stay abreast of international requirements.

2. Though expensive, there is errors and omissions insurance available to travel agencies to protect their agents.

3. Remember that many people don't read. Tell clients what they are supposed to have read. Note on your record that a client was advised.

4. When you do a trip for more than one person, but deal with only one of the persons, note on your records the name of the leader, and when and what you advised that individual. Make that person responsible for transferring the information to the rest of the group. (*Note:* If it is a large group, your safest bet is to have a group meeting and tell everyone the information at the same time.)

Failure to Disclose Information. If you know that the time the client wants to go is at the height of the hurricane season, and you don't mention it for fear of losing the booking, you may be liable if damages occur. If you know that the area is a high-risk place for muggings and thefts, you are responsible for informing clients so they can prepare themselves properly.

How to avoid lawsuits due to failure to disclose information:

1. Keep abreast of political, social, health, and safety occurrences involving tourist destinations, airlines, and cruise ships. You have an obligation as a counsellor to inform clients of any known risks so they can weigh them in making the decision to go or not to go on a particular trip.

2. Ask the tour operator you are dealing with if there have been any recent reports of calamities, mishaps, or tragedies in connection with the places this tour visits. Pass the information on to the client. Note both of these conversations on your client's record. Written records will support the fact that you counselled in a responsible manner.

3. Offer the client travelers' insurance. Keep a written record of issuing the insurance, or of the client's decline of the offer.

DISCLAIMERS

Regardless of who is ultimately at fault if a problem occurs, it is usually the travel agent who is blamed first because this individual is visible, known to the client, and accessible. Therefore, to help protect against some of these claims, agencies often ask a client to sign a disclaimer which releases the agent from certain liabilities. A disclaimer can cover such subjects as rejection of insurance and advising clients of risks. According to lawyers, the disclaimer is not always effective, but if properly handled, it can deter potential lawsuits.

SUMMARY: LIABILITIES

Be careful *what* you say. Never promise that there will be *no* trouble. Even if you are sending clients to orderly, organized Switzerland, do not swear that trains between Geneva and Lucerne *always* run on time. Such statements do nothing except form the basis for a complaint. Finally, make sure that clients have signed up for the trip that they want, and not for the trip that you want them to have.

DEALING WITH THE SEASONED TRAVELER

A client may be extremely knowledgeable about destinations and the art of traveling. Such a person has traveled more than you have, and has more of an understanding of the world and its people than you do. Consequently, you may try to compensate by saying things that make you sound equally experienced and knowledgeable so this client will want to deal with you. Don't.

You can comfortably and successfully handle this client if you keep these things in mind. The best sales strategy with seasoned travelers is to let them have the floor. Allow them to expound on their worldliness. You need simply *react* to the knowledge. Sit up tall; face the client squarely. Look the person in the eye. Nod in affirmation to the monologue and travel requests. If you know for sure that something this client has said is incorrect or that a poor decision has been made, question it indirectly. Don't topple someone's ego by bluntly blurting out the correct information.

Let's say the client has chosen to go to Egypt in the summer because it's so hot here at home. You know that Egypt is even hotter than here. Simply saying so often embarrasses a knowledgeable traveler. Some ways to respond might be:

> "So you can prepare for the trip, let's look at a temperature chart." Pull out a reference guide and present the facts. *Or*, "The desert areas along the Nile do heat up in the summer."

With a seasoned traveler, as with *any* client, incorporate the use of brochures, maps, references, and suppliers as sales aids. Not only will they support you in the sale, they will also establish a more comfortable atmosphere for you.

CONTROLLING THE CONVERSATION

Conversation should be a mutual exchange. You get to know a client by asking questions and by receiving information back. However, some answers get too long-winded and the client does all the talking. Your sales effort has deteriorated from conversation with a purpose to unproductive chatter. It is your responsibility to get the exchange back on track. Two things you can do to control the conversation are:

1. *Remind them why they're talking with you.* They say they want to talk about a week's trip to Germany. They've been there before. So you ask about the places they've been and what they liked about those places. You ask whether they want to go to those cities again or to different ones. They reply that they want to return to one of the cities as a base and travel out into the vicinity.

> Clients: "We just loved Rothenburg. We want to go there again for sure. The first time, we were only there for a few hours. We wandered around in those charming shops, had lunch in a quaint beer house. Managed to drink *two* steins of beer in an hour! We walked along the fortified wall surrounding the city. We met a man who made toys and . . . ."
>
> Counsellor: "Let's take a look at the hotels in Rothenburg and use it as a base." (Grab a hotel reference.)
>
> Client: "My sister broke her hip and I need to get an airline ticket to Detroit so I can help her out. Poor soul. Never been sick a day in her life, and now this. She lives alone. We always told her she should have gotten married. But no, she was always too busy to look for a husband . . . ."
>
> Counsellor: "Since she needs your help now, let's look at the flight schedule for tomorrow morning to Detroit." (Turn to the airline computer and check availability.)

2. *Repeat the client's words.* You can simultaneously get your client's attention and get back into the conversation by using such phrases as "you mentioned," "you said," "you referred to."

> Client: "My son and I are going on a hunting and fishing trip to Mexico alone. I'd like to see what the prices are. He's been bugging me for years to do this. Ever since he was ten and I taught him to shoot, skin, and clean. I heard the peso was good now, so our prices should be cheaper. Love to save money. . . ."
>
> Counsellor: "You said . . . . that your *son* is going with you. If he's under eighteen years old, you'll need a notorized affidavit from his mother granting permission for you to take him to Mexico. Can you get that from her?"
>
> *Or,* "You mentioned . . . the *peso* value is *good.* The tour operators have reduced their package prices in all areas of Mexico. Are you interested in Baja, Yucatan, or elsewhere?"

Stolzenfels Castle, Rhine River, Germany
Photo: Courtesy German Information Center

USING NONVERBAL LANGUAGE

Nonverbal language is an integral part of a sales conversation. In chapter 4 we discussed the instant effect that tone of voice, dress, territory, and touch have on creating rapport and confidence.

We'll now discuss other nonverbal techniques you can use to strengthen your relationship with clients and to direct them in the sales process.

SMILING AND NODDING

Smiling and nodding encourage conversation. If you are a deadpan, clients may think that you are not interested in them or their trip. Remember that vacation counselling deals with emotions. Show some emotion for your client.

EYE CONTACT

Making eye contact will let your client know you are fully engaged in the conversation and not distracted. Look the client in the eye periodically but not for so long that you make the person uncomfortable. If you're constantly looking away, you portray evasiveness and uncertainty.

On the other hand, if you notice the client looking away from you or the brochure too often, the message might be that the discussion isn't interesting. Ask, "How does the cruise sound so far?" The answer should tell you whether to proceed or to shift to another product or destination. (If the answer is "Great, can I take this folder home?" then maybe it's you the client is uncertain about. Have you shown enough confidence in yourself, interest in the client, and knowledge of the subject?)

HAND MOTIONS

When counselling, it is best for several reasons to keep your hands in view. They are then easier to integrate into a demonstration of any point; it's distracting to bring them from hiding to a visible position. Keep your hands reasonably still otherwise. Don't play with your hair or prop up your head.

Don't fold your hands behind your head. This posture is viewed as cocky and arrogant. Especially do not couple this gesture with leaning back in your chair.

It's better to use a pen than your hand to point out information, and you will regularly need a pen to underline and circle items on documents and brochures. So it's a good idea to keep a pen in your hand so you don't have to go looking for it. Just don't click it, twirl it, or drum with it.

SITTING

Sit when the client is sitting. Stand when the client is standing. Remember, you are having a conversation, not giving a lecture.

When you are sitting, be sure to sit up straight and lean toward the client to project your total involvement. Do not get closer than two and a half feet, though, especially when the sale begins.

A good sitting position, provided you are comfortable, is on the edge of your seat. This posture says you're interested and enthusiastic. Use it when you ask for a final approval or toward the end of the sale when you are asking the client to book. It speaks of activity—let's *do* it. Never lean back in your seat or rock backward in the chair. This is a very arrogant position and will hinder communication.

Maori Village, New Zealand
Photo: Courtesy Air New Zealand

REVIEW

SET 1

1. What four common liabilities should counsellors be careful to avoid?

_____

_____

_____

_____

2. What does this sentence mean: The hotel is in walking distance of the shopping district.

_____

_____

3. When counselling, you should keep your hands
   _____ a. on a brochure at all times
   _____ b. in view and in control
   _____ c. in your pockets to keep them still
   _____ d. on your computer ready to make a reservation

SET 2

1. Mr. Sears definitely says that he and his wife want an oceanview room at a beachfront hotel in Jamaica. Give a follow-up conversation about this room request.

_____

_____

_____

_____

_____

_____

2. A client says he wants to plan an around-the-world itinerary with sightseeing excursions in each of eight stops. He says he has done this type of trip twice before and knows what he's doing. Though you have studied foreign destinations, you have not traveled out of the United States yet. What are your sales manners when handling such a well-traveled person?

_____

_____

_____

_____

_____

3. How would you explain to your client that her airline ticket reflects her open jaw as planned between San Francisco and Los Angeles?

_____

_____

_____

_____

SET 3

1. Give some reasons why you might want a client to sign a disclaimer.

_____

_____

_____

_____

_____

2. A client asks you to find her and her husband a hotel in the Mayfair district of London. They want "charm, old-world atmosphere, to pay under $75 a night, and to be near the Hilton." You check your hotel reference guides. You select two properties you feel meet the clients' expectations. You are not personally familiar with these hotels. What do you do to be sure you act properly as a counsellor in order to avoid misrepresentation?

_____

_____

_____

_____

_____

3. Client: "I want you to help me plan a four-week rail trip through Europe in May. I'm planning to go out west to hike the Grand Canyon before July because the first of July I'm moving to Korea to work in a school for a year. I have a busy schedule this year. The school wants me to start in June but I don't know how I can do that." True, you want your customers to tell you their plans, but you also want to sell them their plans. What can you say or do to control the above situation?

_____

_____

_____

_____

_____

7

MATCHING THE PRODUCTS TO THE CLIENT

KEY TERMS
Regular Travel Products
Specialty Travel Products
Budget
Brochure
Penalty Period
Visa
Immigration
Customs

Only after you meet and get to know your client do you proceed to step three in the sales procedure—matching the products to the client. Do not take a shortcut and make this step one, even if the client greets you by saying, "I'd like you to book us on the 15-day trip to England with World Travel departing September 12." Get to know this person before you sell the trip. This does not mean that you are trying to talk someone out of the request or that you are tampering with a definite sale. But it is a counsellor's job to be sure clients have chosen the best product for what they want and expect. So check the client's knowledge of World Travel's trips. Discuss trip expectations with clients and verify that World Travel does, indeed, offer the kind of trip the clients want. You have a far greater chance of selling people the right product if you take at least a few minutes to get to know them. Some conversation time with the client opens up the opportunity for you to sell additional travel products—maybe even better and more expensive ones. If the trip the client has chosen proves to be a good selection, then expectations will be properly met. If the chosen trip proves to be wrong, you have saved the client a great deal of disappointment. Either way, you have most likely gained a repeat customer.

USING DESTINATION GEOGRAPHY

After you thoroughly understand what your client wants and expects in a vacation, you will match those ideas with products and destinations that satisfy. The more you know about products and destinations, the more properly you can suggest vacation choices, and the more quickly you can build an itinerary. You can accumulate destination knowledge in several ways.

Research and read about destinations. Travel as often as you can. When you travel, take notice of the sights and of people's reactions to the sights. Notice the type of people at an attraction: locals or tourists, old or young, formally or informally dressed. Talk to the people at the tourist organizations of the country. Talk to returning travelers. Go to seminars and functions sponsored by suppliers and travel schools. Read the trade press, listen to the news, and read about world events in the newspapers. Maintain an active interest in the world that you sell.

You want to get to the point where you know where the world's countries, cities, seas, and rivers are; where mountains for skiing are; when it is summer in Australia; when it is hurricane season in the Caribbean; which beaches are volcanic; and which reefs offer great diving.

But don't stop there. In order to match your client properly with the right destination and to make sure the trip is enjoyed to the fullest, you will need to point out and describe what there is to see and do at the destination. This "sightseeing" information includes such things as knowing where the Glacier Express train runs; where Notre Dame Cathedral and the Taj Mahal are; how far Versailles is from Paris, and how the tourist can get there by train or bus. It is knowing why a tourist should include Machu Picchu on a tour of Peru, how to get there, how long one should spend there, how massive the ruins are.

Finally, you should be able to describe the people and culture that your client will encounter on the trip, what the languages and religions are, and how the visit may be affected by local customs or attitudes. Tell the client whether the people bargain for goods or use a fixed price system. Provide information about local food, drink, and entertainment that might be of interest.

Wherever your client goes and regardless of the form of travel and the products used, it is advisable to mention that things will be different than they are in the States. That does not make these things wrong, silly, or backward. An accepting attitude about any destination will enhance the cultural experience for your client.

WHEN YOU KNOW ABOUT A DESTINATION

When a client inquires about a destination with which you are familiar, respond briefly. Do not give a lecture to prove that you know Italy. And don't get carried away because it's fun to talk about Italy. You weren't asked for a verbal guidebook on the subject. The client is usually either giving you a little test to see if the two of you will be comfortable together, or simply opening up the conversation. Respond with one or two general sentences, and then ask a question to get more information. Two of the best questions you can ask are: "When do you want to go?" and, "Have you been there before?"

Other destination discussions are opened by clients who give you some information and then ask *you* a question about the proposed trip.

> Clients: "We were in Venice five years ago. We want to go back there, and also visit San Marino, for two weeks in July. Can you talk to us about San Marino?"

Again, do not lecture. Give a few facts and descriptions. Make it a conversation. With the client contributing, you know better what information to cover.

> Counsellor: "San Marino sits high on a bluff crowned with three castles. It has a very storybook look. No vehicles are allowed. The streets are narrow and hilly. Are you looking for charm and romance?"

> Client: "Yes, we do want a place with charm. Even when we shop, we like tiny shops as opposed to department stores. Tell us about the shopping."

WHEN YOU DON'T KNOW ABOUT A DESTINATION

There will be times when a client inquires about a destination with which you're unfamiliar. You needn't readily admit your lack of knowledge unless you are asked pointedly if you know about the area. Remember, you have resources at your finger tips to find answers. To volunteer that you don't know anything about the area may cause a client to lose confidence in you. Maintain client confidence from the beginning by asking the basic questions. Then use your resources (manuals, maps, brochures, other agents in the office). For instance, as you locate Borneo on the map, involve the customer by pointing it out. Or look together at the brochure picture of the Vigeland Park in Oslo.

One situation, however, in which it is acceptable to admit a lack of knowledge is when a client wants to go to a little-known place that you've justifiably never heard of before. Should this situation arise, say that you aren't familiar with the location and ask the client to share with you information about the place. This will not only save the sale, but you also gain knowledge about yet another place in the world.

DESTINATION COMPARISONS

When you are asked to compare two places, again, begin with only a couple of sentences about each place. Get a reaction from the client so you will know how to proceed without wasting everybody's time by giving out unwanted information. Then concentrate on the place in which the customer is more interested.

> Client: "The beaches of Phuket, Thailand and the beaches of Penang, Malaysia receive a lot of publicity. We're trying to decide which one we should go to. Can you help us decide?"

> Counsellor: "You can fly into either place easily. However, the places are different. Phuket has scenery that is very tropical and very beach-oriented. Many areas are quiet, with few people, while Penang is a combination of beach scenery and historical spots. Its beaches are rockier and not very secluded. What kind of beach appeals to you?"

WHEN CLIENTS ASK, "HAVE YOU BEEN THERE?"

Some clients are more secure and trusting if they are talking to a counsellor who has personally traveled to where they want to go. They may feel they'll get more detailed information from a person who has been there personally. So they will ask you, "Have you been there before?"

IF THE ANSWER IS "YES"

If you have been there, tell them "yes," but make only *brief* comments about your visit. They want the assurance that you have been there and know what you are talking about, but they don't want to hear a monologue or see your home movies. End your response with a question to them about their upcoming trip.

> Counsellor: "Yes, I was there for a memorable week in 1985. I was both in Rio and up in the mountains. Are you thinking about staying in Rio for the whole week?"

They are interested in what's going to happen in *their* dream, not what happened in yours. Therefore, convert as many of your personal travel experiences as possible into counselling advice. If you shopped for precious jewelery in Rio and learned that the Brazilian bargaining practice is to play one merchant off another, then relay this tidbit as advice based on your knowledge of Brazil, rather than simply your particular experience.

Note the following two examples:

> Counsellor: "Do you plan to buy precious jewelry? If so, *you'll* get a better price from a merchant if *you* say that the merchant next door offers this aquamarine ring for less than he does. And he should bargain down. If *you*

don't like his deal, start out the door for the next merchant. The shopkeeper will probably stop *you* and come down in price."

Counsellor: "When *I* bought my aquamarine ring, *I* priced it at one shop, thought it should be less expensive, so *I* went to the next merchant. *I* asked him if he could do any better than next door . . . ."

IF THE ANSWER IS "NO"

How do you keep your clients' confidence when you haven't visited the place they want to go? *Be honest. Give evidence of knowledge obtained in some other manner.* You want them to realize that as a travel professional you gain knowledge in myriad [*miriad*] ways. They need not be nervous about your abilities.

număr extrem de mare

Counsellor: "No; however, I have studied and arranged many trips to the destination. And I have the resources to get any special information that you want about the city."

REGULAR AND SPECIALTY TRAVEL PRODUCTS

Travel products fall into two main categories: *regular* and *specialty*. A thorough understanding of these on your part will better enable you to match a product to the client.

In the regular category are those trips that provide the *highlights* of a city, country, place, even of a museum or cathedral. They cover those things that the average tourist wants to see and experience. The 15-day air-conditioned motorcoach tour of Scandinavia that includes sightseeing in Helsinki, Oslo, Stockholm, and Copenhagen is a regular trip.

In the specialty category are those trips that go into more depth, explore less traveled areas, expose the traveler to the uniqueness of the people and the place, and/or cater to special interests and particular requests. The 15-day specialty trip to Scandinavia might include a snowmobile safari to a reindeer herder's inn in Finnish Lapland and a cruise of the Norwegian fjords.

Keep in mind that what separates the two categories is not price, quality, form of travel, or type of trip. Both offer a variety of choices—from budget to deluxe, and from escorted to independent. The sole distinguishing factor is the depth of involvement of the traveler with the local culture or with a special interest.

About eighty percent of travelers are interested in regular trips that *sample* the food, drink, and entertainment of a particular locale, but do not provide them as daily fare. A regular traveler wants to see the people and observe their activities and customs, but does not want to mingle with them as intimately as do specialty travelers. A regular traveler wants to "do" Europe on this vacation.

The other twenty percent of travelers, on the other hand, either want to understand and participate in local customs, eat all of the local foods, and experience as closely as possible everything that culture has to offer, or they are seeking to satisfy a specialized interest such as rock collecting or scuba diving in a remote spring or lake.

HANDLING THIRD-PARTY RECOMMENDATIONS

Sometimes a customer comes to you with a destination or product recommendation made by a friend or relative. She says that her neighbors went on the *Sea Mermaid* cruise and loved it; therefore, they recommend that she go on it and they know she'll love it. So she tells you that she definitely wants to book a cabin for the July 10 sailing. Your first thought may be that this is a quick sale. Why spend any time with this woman when she knows what she wants? However, you should spend time with her because it is your responsibility to guide your client to her best choice of the vacation that will provide what she's looking for.

How do you know what she's looking for in a vacation if you haven't questioned her about it yet? How do you know that this particular cruise is right for her if you don't know what she means by a "great cruise"? If you don't find out that information before you make a sale you may regret it, because if the cruise ends up being an ill-suited product, the customer will look to you to make amends because you sold the product to her. She does not turn to the friend who recommended it.

Reindeer Safari, Finnish Lapland
Photo: Courtesy Finnish Tourist Board

A most important initial query to the customer, therefore, is, "Have you been on a cruise [or whatever] before?" If the answer is "yes," then find out about her experience with cruises. (*Note:* You are not trying to talk her out of the sale. You are simply determining if the present recommendation is a good selection.)

> Counsellor: "Which ship were you on? When? What did you like about it? Do you want something similar or different from that cruise?"

If the answer, though, is "no," then ask a different set of questions.

> Counsellor: "What attracts you to cruising? What specifically did your friend like about the cruise? Do you feel the same way?"

Whatever the answers are, make sure they are compatible to the cruise ship she has selected. Let the customer know.

If you feel that a second product choice needs to be presented, explain why. Seek the customer's agreement to look at an alternate.

DISCUSSING BUDGETS

Knowing how much someone is able and willing to spend for a vacation is a key factor in matching the client with the right product. However, don't bring up the question of money right away—it may appear that your greatest interest is not the client, but how much you are going to make off the trip. So wait a bit. Get answers to who, what, when, where, how, and why before you ask *how much*. By doing this, you and the client will become more comfortable with each other and you will arrive at a clearer understanding of what the client is looking for in a vacation. When the question of money does come up, things should go smoothly, and at this point most clients will give you a clear and accurate estimate of how much they are willing to spend.

But not all clients, alas. For it is in the area of money more than any other that a client is apt to be vague or unrealistic. There are several reasons for this, and it is important to keep in mind that the client isn't being evasive just for the sake of being difficult. In the client's mind, there are good reasons for not giving you an accurate estimate of what will be spent.

It may be that the person doesn't want to quote you a price for fear that it will be so ridiculously low as to make the client appear cheap or naïve. Or clients may not want to tell you how much they're willing to spend because they're afraid you'll take advantage of them and sell them more than they need. Other buyers may begin the sales transaction by asking for the "least expensive" (even though this isn't really what they want) because they think this is a good way to "bargain." Still other clients—the type you will encounter often—will want to see what a particular tour offers before telling you what they want to spend. (These clients are more interested in what they're getting than what they have to spend. Show them what they want and they will usually find the money for it.)

When dealing with clients like these, a good technique to use is to ask for (or even suggest) a budget range, rather than a specific figure. Clients are more apt to respond to a request of this kind because it does not pin them down or commit them to a definite figure. They still have "room to maneuver."

Asking for a budget range is also a good way to find out if the quote is more than the client really wants to spend, or, more often, if the figure given really is less than what the client is willing to spend.

> Client: "Oh, we'd like to spend about $5,000 for the both of us."

> Counsellor: "About $5,000–7,000?"

If the client answers with a flat "yes," or "yes, about that," then you are probably safe in staying on the high side of $5,000. If the answer is "yes, about $5,000," then stay close to that figure. If the answer is "yes, about that, maybe a little less," probe further. The client really may be thinking "$3,000–4,000." If so, asking "$4,000–5,000" and so on will ultimately get you on the right wavelength.

Other types of clients who may, quite unintentionally, pose a problem when it comes time to discuss money are those buyers who give you an unrealistic estimate because they don't have an accurate idea of what travel products cost. They describe their dream trip to you and then, at the end, say that they have budgeted $1,500 for it. When you tell them that they are looking at $5,000 minimum, such clients may be embarrassed, or even crestfallen. Don't just say, "Sorry," and send them on their way. Work with these clients. Suggest alternatives. Show them what $1,500 *will* buy. If you don't, then rest assured that another agent in another office will.

Should you encounter any of the above, or similar, situations (and you will), keep two things in mind. One, you can lose a sale if you dismiss a client as a serious buyer simply because you didn't get a satisfactory answer right away to how much the person plans to spend. Two, you can limit a sale if you prejudge a client's financial status too quickly, or take as gospel the first estimate.

DISCUSSING COSTS

The bitterness of poor quality lasts long after the sweetness of low price.
Author unknown

When you discuss costs with a client, be candid and thorough. If you don't make sure your client completely understands the costs involved in the trip, it could come back to haunt you in the form of a dissatisfied client, or in your agency having to pick up a tab that the client refuses to pay because the person claims that you never mentioned it.

Generally, there are three types of costs that you may be discussing with a client, depending upon the services you're providing and the products you're selling. These are professional fees, service charges, and product costs.

Professional fees are those costs charged by an agency for counselling time. Not all agencies levy a professional fee for counselling, but many do, and those that do may levy them in a variety of ways. That is, they may charge a flat fee, or they may charge by the hour, the destination, the project, or the length of the trip. Should a client book with that agency, the fee may either be added to the product costs, or applied against the costs of the trip. Regardless of the agency's method, it is essential that the counsellor discuss this fee *early* in the conversation. Have these charges posted on a sign, or listed on paper distributed individually to clients, or both. Be clear about these fees, and about how and when they are paid. Do not be apologetic or wimpy. It is a fair exchange—money for services.

Service charges are those costs charged by some agencies for such matters as cancellations, ticket rewrites, long distance phone calls, or visa assistance. Like professional fees, they should be discussed early in the conversation, posted on a sign, and given to the client in printed form.

Product costs are the charges for hotels, cars, tours, cruises and the like as stated in the brochure or as negotiated, *plus* any taxes and service charges that are to be added on. These should be discussed *late* in the conversation. Remember, you've gotten to know your client so you have probably selected products that are within the stated budget range. If you get clients excited about the trip first, the cost for what they want is accepted more quickly with fewer objections.

When discussing a price given in the brochure, be sure to tell the client all the features that are covered in the price, e.g., air fare, hotel room, meals, and rental car, even if these features are clearly listed in the brochure. This will tell clients what they're getting, and, by omission, what they're not getting. They may have been expecting breakfast. If you don't mention it, the client will. This process clears up such misconceptions.

Next, go over any and all taxes and service charges that the client will be responsible for. These could be state taxes, maid service fees, or even air-conditioning charges. If not already included in the brochure price, they can add as much as thirty-five percent to the stated cost of the client's trip. If taxes and service charges are included in the brochure price, say so. If they are not, let the client know right away how much extra they will be, and whether the client is to pay you for these charges, or pay them to the individual suppliers while on the trip. Don't neglect to cover these even if the client won't be paying you for them and you won't be getting anything from them. For example, a client may think that a five-night hotel stay has been prepaid in full, only to be presented upon check-out with a bill for $40–$50 for taxes and $15 for maid service. No conscientious counsellor would subject a client to this kind of vacation shock.

Another area in which you want to eliminate any unpleasant surprises for your client concerns change fees and cancellation penalties imposed by the supplier. If the client wishes to change an item in a booked trip, that is, to change hotels, add or subtract a member of the party, or change the duration of the trip, the supplier may charge a fee to do so. Similarly, if a client decides to cancel a trip for whatever reason, the supplier reserves the right to refund all, none, or only a portion of the client's money, depending on when the cancellation is made. Most suppliers will make a complete refund if a cancellation is made prior to the supplier's *penalty period,* which is a specified number of hours or days before the product is used. If cancellation falls within this penalty period the supplier will refund only a portion or none of the money.

Make sure that you apprise your client of these charges *before* you are paid any money rather than after, or when the client decides to cancel. (*Note:* Insurance is available to cover these contingencies.)

Keep in mind, however, that the supplier holds the agency, not the client, responsible for any cancellation penalties, *whether or not* the client has paid the agency for the booking. Therefore, be sure that you collect for any booking that you have made *before* it enters the penalty period, or cancel the booking. Should a client wish to book *during* a penalty period, either collect the money before calling the supplier, or at the very least get a credit card number from the client. This will protect you should the client cancel.

COST VARIANCES

Total product costs can vary depending on such things as season of the year one travels, a single traveler booking instead of two, three sharing a cabin instead of two, or traveling during a holiday period. Such variances usually carry an extra charge called a "supplement." Tell the client about the supplement and then include it in the total cost.

Cost variances are also found in package tours that offer choices of hotels or other features. For example, a client going to Orlando may choose from a list of ten hotels or may choose tickets for Disney World and Epcot or just for Epcot. The choices will affect the cost.

TALKING DISCOUNTS

We tend to think in terms of dollars, not percentages. Dollars are concrete, percentages are abstract. Therefore, when you sell travel products that are on sale, quote the savings in dollars. It will have more meaning to your clients. Tell them that they save $60 if they stay over Saturday night. Tell them that if they put a deposit on the Alaska cruise by March first, they will save $200 on that cabin. You have a better chance of making a sale if you do.

WORKING WITH BROCHURES

A brochure is one of your most important sales tools. It provides both you and the client with a visual and verbal description of the vacation product, and it furnishes you with all the fine details regarding costs, schedules, and itineraries. You won't be able to become thoroughly familiar with each and every brochure before showing them to your client, but you certainly should become familiar with the general format of brochures and the most effective way of presenting them to a client.

Most brochures have three main parts. Knowing what is in each part will enable you to turn more easily to the appropriate section to answer a client's question and to make a step-by-step presentation of the product, whether it is a hotel, a tour, a cruise, or even a car rental.

The first part of the brochure describes the product and gives the supplier's qualifications. This section attempts to entice, to convince, to excite, and to whet the client's appetite. A hotel brochure will have pictures of the rooms, the grounds, the restaurant, and a write-up of the hotel's features. A tour brochure will show the hotels used, the escorts employed, the bus company used, and the special events included. A cruise brochure will show onboard activities and onshore sights.

The second section lists the various prices, options, and selections available to the client. Included here are rates, activities, itineraries, deck plans, and a detailed list of what is and is not provided at each rate.

The third part, usually located at the back of the brochure, contains all the "fine print," often called "terms and conditions." This part is concerned with deposit money, final payment, cancellations, insurance, baggage, booking change, and responsibilities of the operator.

Most brochures use this three-part format. However, some smaller brochures may combine certain sections, and, increasingly, some companies are putting cost/ price information on a separate sheet to be used in conjunction with the brochure. This effectively keeps cost information from the client until you are ready to discuss it. And, because prices change so frequently, it allows the supplier simply to print a new price schedule without having to reprint the whole brochure.

Brochures vary widely in quality and in the amount of information they contain. As a general rule, the more questions the brochure can answer for you the better the brochure, because less time needs to be spent searching for answers and the more quickly and smoothly the sale will go. Therefore, select travel companies whose brochures are thorough and easy to use. Usually these are the better companies.

To begin, bring out only one or two brochures for discussion. More than that confuses the customer. Have in view and talk about only one brochure at a time, even if several represent the same travel company. Keep your hands on the brochure; keep a pen in your hand for pointing, or a marker for highlighting. (If the brochure has an index, use it to locate the section you need. Don't flip the pages in a clumsy search.)

Control the brochure during the presentation period. Direct the customer through the pages and the itinerary. Say first what *you* think this person needs to know about the itinerary. Otherwise the customer tends to wander aimlessly, causing wasted time and no sale because of lack of direction. Place the brochure between you and the client so you can both see it easily. Or have it face the client if you can spot-read main words upside down or know the layout well.

Counseller: "This itinerary with Traveling Times is fifteen days [point] which is the time you are planning. It does make a day's stop in Florence which you want to do [point or mark]. The rate is within your budget [point]. And it does have a departure during your preferred weeks of vacation [mark it]."

As you point and mark, your customer's attention will be focused on what you are showing. Seek the client's approval regularly during your presentation.

Counseller: "How do you like this itinerary? Does this itinerary go to all the places you're interested in? How does this sound so far? Is there anything this tour doesn't have that you would like it to have?"

If the answer to your questions is "no," don't waste any more time on that company or itinerary. Check out another selection. If another brochure needs to be looked at, set the first one aside and out of sight.

When a selection has been finalized, give the client the brochure that you have circled and underlined for the trip. This copy becomes the client's personal property.

If a client stops in briefly and asks for brochures but doesn't have time to discuss them, give out only one or two brochures on each subject in which interest has been expressed. That is enough for someone to begin an investigation. Don't just hand them over. If possible, try to build a little rapport by giving the person a concise fact about each brochure, holding each appropriate brochure in turn toward the customer as you do so. For this client, who professes no time to stay, you've said enough. Get the person's name and phone number; present your business card. Make a note to yourself about the brochures you gave the customer. And call later to discuss them further.

USING TRAVEL VIDEO

Travel videos are another excellent sales tool, and they are available on a wide variety of products and destinations. Video adds to the client/agent interaction. However, they are not a substitute for the personal contact and involvement that a counsellor provides, and showing them can be time consuming. Therefore, use video with discretion. And remember, not all prospects hesitate to buy. For that reason videos are an extra sales aid, not a necessary one.

Here are some reasons you might show a video to a prospect:

- You judge that the client doesn't seem to believe what you are saying. Use video to lend credibility to your recommendations.

- You feel you haven't created sufficient interest for the client to buy. Video can set the mood and generate appropriate vacation feelings.

- You see that the prospect seems to vacillate or seems to be getting confused from all the information in the brochure. Video helps to focus attention on the suggestion(s).

- Clients give you an ultimatum that, say, a cruise better be right for them. Showing a video can reduce liability by assuring that these clients have an accurate idea of what their vacation will be like.

- You need to show a client verification that what you say is correct. Seeing a video about the product instills greater trust.

- You've answered all questions but the client doesn't seem ready to buy. Use video to help close the sale.

If you deem a video necessary, tell (don't ask) the client that you're going to show a video. State what it's about and how long it lasts. Don't just say, "Watch this."

The time frame that seems to work best is a five- to twelve-minute viewing. With anything longer, enthusiasm drops off. If you are showing a video for any reason to a single customer, stay for the entire viewing. If there are two or more clients, leave them alone, at least for the first few minutes, so they can discuss it among themselves. *Be sure to be there when the video ends.* When it's over be prepared with a statement linking the video to your discussion with them before the viewing.

DISCUSSING INTERNATIONAL REQUIREMENTS

When matching products to the client, you must include counselling on international requirements and procedures. You want to guarantee that the traveler will experience little or no inconvenience when crossing international boundaries. To assure this, it is necessary that the individual possess credentials such as passport, visa, tourist card, money declarations, onward ticket, and/or immunization record that permits travelers to leave one country, enter another, and return to the United States. If any of the required documents is missing or is prepared improperly, the long awaited dream trip could come to a screeching halt. Which documents are needed varies widely from country to country, depending on the status of the traveler, the purpose of the visit, and the length of stay. Because document requirements can change overnight, it is important that you always check, for each passenger, what the current rules are. Also, be sure to check them during the initial counselling session so there will be plenty of time to obtain the necessary documents.

Where do you find a list of the entry/exit requirements by country? You have several sources at your fingertips in any travel office.

- Travel Planners. Use the North American, European, or Pacific planner depending on the country in question.

- *Pan Am's World Guide.* This is an encyclopedia of travel issued by Pan American World Airways. It contains not only entry requirements, but a wealth of other valuable information, such as country statistics, airport information, accommodations, what to see, food and restaurants, sports, shopping, drinking tips, entertainment, and helpful hints for traveling in each country. *Pan Am's USA Guide* is also available.

- Airline Computer. Documentation information is stored in all airline reservations computer systems.

- *Pan Am Immigration Guide.* This is a comprehensive manual that gives explicit instructions on how travelers and their possessions are to enter and exit a country.

- Consulates and Tourist Offices. International entry/exit requirements can be obtained directly from the consulate and tourist offices of the appropriate country. The addresses and phone numbers of their United States locations are in the travel planners.

- Visa Services. These organizations specifically handle travel documentation on travelers' behalf. There is a fee for using this service. Visa service names, addresses, and phone numbers are in each of the planners.

VISAS

A *visa* is an endorsement issued by a consulate or other government office that gives the holder permission to enter that country. The endorsement is stamped or stapled in a passport, or, in very special cases (usually when traveling between two warring nations), issued on a piece of paper and kept separate from the passport. There are several types of visas. The two that you will most commonly deal with are the *tourist visa,* issued to those who plan to stay in a country for visiting purposes, and the *transit visa,* issued to those whose stay is less than three days with the intent of continuing on to another country. Others that you may deal with are work, business, student, and immigration visas.

HOW TO OBTAIN A VISA

Your clients may ask you to obtain their visas for them, or prefer to do it themselves. They may *have* to do it themselves because certain countries require that travelers obtain their visas at the point of entry into the country. (*Note:* Some agencies prefer not to handle visas and don't provide this service.)

The procedure for getting a visa on behalf of your client is:

Step 1: Call or write the consulate or visa service representing the particular country and request a visa application.

Step 2: Have your client fill out the application. The application may need to be supported with passport-type photos, money, a copy of the airline ticket verifying onward transportation, evidence of financial responsibility, and/or a certificate of vaccination. Business visas often require even more, such as a letter of invitation and character references.

Step 3: Mail the application, the required supporting materials, *and the passport,* either to a visa service or directly to the consulate. The passport is always submitted with the application because the visa endorsement is either stamped in the passport or stapled to one of the pages.

Step 4: If the application is accepted, the consulate returns the passport and visa by mail.

WHY USE A VISA SERVICE?

You can get quicker service by sending the visa application via a visa service company instead of to the foreign consulate directly. The visa service saves you time and trouble by making sure that the application is correct before submission, and by literally walking the application through. Otherwise, the request may sit on the consul's desk without receiving immediate attention. If your client needs visas for more than one country, it is another plus to send the applications to one visa service, which will walk each one through the appropriate consulate and mail the complete package of visas back to you.

Visas can take anywhere from one to six weeks to be processed. Start early. Some countries charge for visas; visa services always have a fee.

TOURIST CARDS

Some countries, notably Mexico and countries in Central and South America, require a *tourist card* instead of a visa for entry. This is a simple, easy to obtain document registering the incoming traveler. It helps countries keep a tally of who is visiting, for how long, when, and why. Depending on the country, it can be obtained through the consulate, the tourist board office, or the airline. Some countries distribute the forms to travel agencies which can then issue them to clients. Most of them are free or bear a nominal charge.

IMMUNIZATIONS

It is your responsibility to advise a traveler about immunizations that may be required before entering a country that has diseases such as cholera, yellow fever, malaria, and polio. Countries without these diseases may also require the immunizations if the traveler has been in an infected area prior to arrival. Because health situations can change by the week, and because it's difficult to keep up to date with global infections, various health organizations may recommend immunizations in addition to the required ones. Strongly suggest to your clients that they get the recommended immunizations as well as the required ones.

Some immunizations, in order to be effective, need to be got as much as six weeks prior to entering an infected country. Therefore, *check documentary requirements for these health precautions at the initial counselling session.*

The traveler must obtain as proof of immunization a yellow booklet called the International Certificate of Vaccination, which is officially recognized the world over. The booklet must be signed by the health facility or private physician that administered the immunization.

ARRIVAL AT POINT OF ENTRY

Some travelers, especially novices, are nervous about what to do when entering or leaving a country. A good counsellor will ease this tension by explaining the various procedures.

Advise your client that there are two required steps for entering any country: 1) The traveler must proceed first and immediately to *immigration* which checks *people*. Here the immigration officer will check passport and all other required documentation for entry to be sure it's all in order. 2) The traveler then proceeds, by following the signs, to baggage claim. (*Note:* It's a good idea to familiarize your client with international airport signs. These are in the travel planners.) After travelers pick up their luggage, they take it to *customs* which inspects *baggage*.

LEAVING A VISITED COUNTRY

When leaving the visited country, the traveler checks in at the airline counter, where documents are reviewed. Sometimes they are examined again as the traveler enters the international departure hall.

There is often an extra procedure or stop to make, *to pay airport taxes*. Many countries (including the U.S.) have what is called an airport tax or a departure tax. This tax is usually paid in local currency. Advise your client in advance how much it will be so the appropriate amount of money can be set aside. You will find a chart in the *Worldwide OAG* listing all the countries that require taxes and how much the taxes are.

RETURNING TO THE UNITED STATES

Before the plane lands in the United States, the flight attendants will hand each person a *customs declaration* form to fill out. The traveler is to list on this form what was purchased on the trip and is being carried back into the U.S. Remind your clients, especially if they plan to shop a lot, to keep their receipts together in a carry-on for ease of checking in at customs.

Tell your clients that after the plane lands, they are to proceed immediately to U.S. Immigration, then on to baggage claim, and then directly through customs. Each traveler is allowed to bring back $400 worth of goods duty free (no tax will be paid on these items) if

- Articles are for personal use or gifts.

- Articles accompany the passenger.

- The passenger has been out of the country at least forty-eight hours. Mexico and the U.S. Virgin Islands are exempt from the forty-eight-hour limitation.

- A passenger has not declared this exemption in the past thirty days.

If the person is returning from a trip that includes Guam, U.S. Virgin Islands, or American Samoa, the duty free amount doubles to $800.

Some articles cannot be brought into the U.S., such as ivory, turtle products, and plants. For clients who need more details, refer them to the U.S. Customs Service in Washington, D.C., or obtain copies of the pamphlet "Pocket Hints" (customs publication no. 506).

RECOMMENDING TRAVEL ASSISTANCE AND INSURANCE

You can sell both travel assistance and travel insurance to your customers, and it is recommended that you do so. These protect your clients and you against unforeseen problems with the products, as well as problems with baggage, health, and local occurrences.

Travel assistance provides on-site help in the midst of a travel emergency. Depending on the company, coverage may include emergency evacuation, a credit line, interpreter service, 24-hour hot line, and legal aid.

Travel insurance, on the other hand, covers some or much of the cost of an emergency, but after the fact. The several kinds of coverage available include accidental death and dismemberment, medical expenses for illness and injury, trip cancellation and interruption, and baggage.

Consider selling travel assistance/insurance to everyone, but especially to senior citizens, to those who already have health problems, to those going to volatile locations, to adventure travelers, and to those who just worry a lot.

Other than protection, there are two more reasons for selling assistance/insurance or at least asking clients to buy it: 1) the travel agency receives a commission as high as thirty-five percent for all assistance/insurance sold, and 2) if something goes wrong that travel assistance/insurance will recoup or protect, chances for agency liability are lessened. Be sure to note on customers' reservation records that you suggested insurance, and note whether they purchased the insurance or declined the recommendation.

What if the clients say that they already have insurance? Tell them to check their policies to be sure what is and isn't covered. Check whether it provides enough coverage to handle international expenses, and whether it includes coverage for incidents outside the United States.

As a vacation counsellor, your responsibility is to suggest insurance to clients, and tell them why they need it. However, remember that you're a counsellor, not an insurance agent. It's the client's responsibility to read and understand the policy. You're not expected to, nor should you, expound at length on the fine details of the policy. Any claims against the policy will be worked out between the insurance company and the clients. At most, you should be asked only to contribute supporting documents.

REVIEW

SET 1

1. Describe what you find in each of the three parts of a tour/cruise brochure.

   _____

   _____

   _____

2. Explain the difference between a visa and a tourist card.

   _____

   _____

   _____

3. What is immigration responsible for checking? What is customs responsible for checking?

   _____

4. When should you discuss professional fees and service charges with clients? When should you discuss product costs with clients?

   _____

   _____

   _____

5. When showing a video in your office, what is the most effective length of viewing time?

   _____

6. What is the International Certificate of Vaccination?

_____

_____

_____

SET 2

1. Give a profile of a person who wants to buy regular travel products.

_____

_____

_____

2. Explain why asking for a "budget range" produces a more accurate result than asking for a "budget."

_____

_____

_____

_____

3. Why should clients buy travel insurance? Why should you encourage them to buy insurance?

_____

_____

_____

4. Why should you, not the customer, control the brochure during the sales presentation?

_____

_____

_____

_____

SET 3

1. Client: "Can I get all your brochures on Italy? My friend is in the car waiting for me. We'll come back later when we have time to talk with you." What should you say and do?

_____

_____

_____

_____

_____

_____

_____

_____

2. Your clients seem to need verification of what you're saying. You show them an appropriate video to reassure them. Should you watch it with them or leave them alone? Why?

_____

_____

_____

3. Client: "I need to make arrangements for a trip to Beijing and Shangdong Province in China. Have you been there?" What are some acceptable responses a) if you have been there, and b) if you haven't?

a. _____

_____

_____

_____

b. _____

_____

_____

_____

8

OVERCOMING OBJECTIONS

A client may have an objection to a trip before you even start your presentation. Another client may get stuck trying to answer one of the basic questions, such as *when*. And others won't object to a thing until you ask them to book what you've been discussing for the last two hours! Is there any way to predict what these objections might be and when they are most likely to occur? Yes. Keep in mind, though, that objections are to be welcomed because they keep the lines of communication open. A client expressing an objection is also indicating a desire for a resolution. Answering the objection moves the sale forward.

RECOGNIZING COMMON OBJECTIONS AND HANDLING THEM

There are many obvious objections. But there are times when the stated objection is hiding the real one. For help in deciding which is which, notice any mixed signals. Does the client say that the date is wrong while looking around your office at all the posters of other places in the world? Ask a blunt question, such as, "If I locate a similar tour with your preferred departure date, will you buy it?" If the client hesitates, there may be other objections the person is not yet willing to share with you. Let's list some of the common objections and some suggestions for resolving them.

1. *Objections to the Product.* It's too long, the hotels are wrong, there's not enough nightlife, it doesn't include a particular city of interest, the dates are wrong.

> Client: "The itinerary doesn't include San Marino which we're really interested in."

> Counsellor: "There is a tour operator that does include San Marino in their Italy tours. I'll go get it from the back room. Just a minute."

Suggested Solution: Offer an alternative. Immediately. Try not to have any lag time. Get the brochure immediately. If the client objects, then the stated objection may not be the real one.

2. *Objections to Price.* It's too expensive.

> Client: "This tour costs more than we want to spend."

> Counsellor: "The cost is in line with the types of hotels that are centrally located, which you indicated is important. And they do use the best tour managers which is important when traveling in this part of the world. Are you really willing to give up these comforts and securities for a lower price?"

Suggested Solution: Most people are not willing to give them up. So don't agree right away. If you have listened to a client's needs earlier in the conversation, then you have selected an appropriate tour. Clients simply want to be sure they aren't spending more money than necessary. If the answer to the question about trading comfort and security for price is "yes," then you know the stated objection is a legitimate one; show the client a lower-priced tour. Point out the differences between the original selection and the lower priced one. The client may appreciate these differences and stay with the original. If the alternative is chosen, you've still resolved the objection. Even if you feel that the alternative is not as suitable, you did present the differences and the customer made the choice.

3. *Objections to the Tour Company.* Never heard of this company. Are they any good?

You, not the client, are in the travel business. It is quite likely that someone has not heard of the tour company. Not all operators advertise in the public media. That does not mean they are not good. As long as you've selected a reputable company, you needn't back down to this objection.

Suggested Solution: Assure your client that the company does offer a quality product. If possible, give references; say that your other clients have been on this tour and have been pleased.

4. *Objections to Commitment.* The client wants to think it over.

Suggested Solution: It's okay to be blunt with clients on this one. What are they uncertain about? What did you say that now makes them hesitate? A client just may come up with a real objection which you can clear up. Or, if they have a legitimate need to "sleep on it," then offer to call tomorrow for the answer.

5. *Objections to Paying.* When they have the money, they'll book it!

These people may be afraid of commitment. The objection doesn't have anything to do with money.

Suggested Solution: Tell them that it is best to confirm what they want now, while it's available, and that if they change their minds later they can always cancel and get their money back. However, if their objection does stem from a legitimate concern for money, tell them that at this point they simply need to put a deposit down to insure that they will go on vacation this year. They have time to pay the bulk of the money later, and you can help them work out a time-payment plan if need be.

6. *Objections to making the decision alone.* The client has to consult with a spouse or babysitter or other member of the traveling group.

Suggested Solution: There's not much you can do to overcome this type of objection. Accept it. Just be sure that the present party leaves feeling optimistic and convinced and ready to go. Offer to phone at a set later date to answer any questions that have come up. Try to make an appointment for this party to bring the other partners in to finalize the plans.

RECOGNIZING QUESTIONS THAT ARE OBJECTIONS

Two girls want to go to Honolulu for a week. They don't have a lot of money, they tell you, but they are willing to "go cheap." Your selection is an inexpensive package that includes round-trip air fare, a hotel two blocks off the beach for seven nights, transfers, and one sightseeing tour.

These girls keep stressing price, so you keep reminding them what a great price deal this is. You're pleased that they will get their dream of being in Hawaii. Then they query:

> Clients: "You say that this hotel is two blocks off the beach?"
>
> Counsellor: "Yes."

You may be thinking that they just want an affirmation of the information or assurance that they heard you right. But this question is actually an objection. They had no idea what they would have to accept in order to "go cheap." These girls really want the instant action of Waikiki Beach. Two blocks off the beach is not acceptable to them. But what about price? It's not the main concern anymore. If you don't catch this, and question it, their final response usually will be something like:

> Clients: "Could we take this brochure home? We'd like to talk about it with another friend. We'll get back to you."

Indeed, they will think about it. And then they'll go to another agent to see what packages with hotels *on the beach* that agency has to offer. Of course, you have those packages too. But you didn't bother to show an alternative because they didn't ask for it! Or did they?

Next time a client reiterates a fact in the form of a question, pursue the reason.

> Counsellor: "Yes, to keep your price down involves staying two blocks off the beach. How do you feel about not being right *on the beach?*"

Watch their expressions as well as listen to their response.

> Girls: "Well, . . . this is a beach vacation . . . ."

> Counsellor: "True! Let's look at a standard room rate at a first class hotel on the beach. Trade off; pay a bit more for the hotel on the beach and eat at McDonalds for breakfast every morning instead of in the hotel restaurant."

> Clients: "That's an idea. What are some other ways we could save money in exchange for a better-located hotel?"

Not only do you make more commission, but these clients actually get what they want. And they appreciate you more as a counsellor. They are more likely to use your services again.

Some objections come in the form of fear or distrust. If not allayed immediately, these feelings could cancel out the booking about to be made or one that has already been confirmed.

In the next example, the agent has already closed the sale, a 7-day Caribbean cruise departing this weekend. The agent is explaining what happens next. At this point, the client has an objection.

> Agent: "Because of the lack of mailing time between today and Saturday, your airline ticket will be waiting for you at the Delta counter at the airport. Your cruise ticket will be waiting for you at the pier."

> Client: "You say my cruise ticket will be waiting at the pier?"

This client may be afraid that the ticket won't be there. To allay this fear, explain the procedure in detail. Explain that a pier pick-up is normal practice. "There is a special window marked pier pick-up. Ask for the tickets by your name and proceed aboard . . . ."

If you do not give more information this passenger could decide not to take the cruise at all. Illogical? If uneasy about this situation, a client might imagine other things not going well either.

WHEN CLIENTS ARGUE WITH EACH OTHER

Some objections occur for reasons that have nothing to do with either you or the product. Clients might begin an argument between themselves as soon as you meet them.

>Mrs. White to counsellor: "We'd like to talk to you about going on a cruise."

>Mr. White to Mrs. White: "Cruise? I thought we were going to Europe."

When this happens, make a statement that will appease both of them. Or that will at least focus their attention on you. Then you can start from the beginning by asking them appropriate questions.

>Counsellor: "How about a European cruise? Or a cruise to Europe and then a motorcoach tour? Let's discuss your options."

(*Note:* Yes, we did start out by suggesting a product in the first step. We did that simply to get the clients untangled. Once they are focused on you, proceed to give a normal presentation. The sale may end up being a cruise to Europe. But you must back up and go through the sales procedure to find out.)

If clients begin to argue *during* the presentation, evaluate the situation; no two instances are alike. Judge whether to intervene or not.

For instance, a couple begins to argue about how much to spend for the trip. One partner grows silent. You may judge *not* to intervene, sensing that the problem will not be discussed openly with you sitting there. So the argument won't be resolved. Shortly, one of the clients says, "We'll have to think about it; we'll call you later." Embarrassment often keeps such people from returning to your agency. The potential sale has been lost.

If you choose not to intervene, get out of the clients' way for a couple of minutes. Give a simple reason to leave them alone to debate, such as finding them another brochure. Once you give a reason to leave, get up and go immediately. When you return, continue where you left off. You may or may not need to use that new brochure.

But if you do decide to intervene, stay there and contribute to the debate by adding additional information. Let's say one client wants to stay in Rome for three days and then go down to Pompeii for a day by train or by local bus. The traveling partner does not want to spend vacation time hurrying from place to place trying to figure out where they're supposed to be.

You can help these people solve their debate by interjecting needed information:

> Counsellor: "You both have good ideas. You could go down to Pompeii, but it's true that public transportation would have to be figured out and the schedules are not feasible for the amount of time you have. However, there is something you could do to satisfy you both. [pause] There are organized tours that take you to Pompeii. You sit comfortably on the motorcoach traveling directly to Pompeii absorbing the scenery along the way. Here's a Grayline tour . . . ."

Why the pause? Remember that you are witnessing an argument, regardless of how polite it seems. You need to gain control. The pause makes the clients pay attention to you and to what comes next.

As a counsellor you will make judgments all the time. No suggestion will work all the time. Just have some tricks in your bag. It's up to you to decide which one to pull out and when.

REVIEW

SET 1

1. Name two common objections to buying a vacation that clients might raise.

_____

_____

2. If clients object to a product, what can you do?

_____

_____

SET 2

1. Why should you welcome rather than fear objections from prospective clients?

_____

_____

2. What body language should you use when confronted with objections?

_____

_____

_____

3. Why might some people ask you a question that is actually a repeat of the answer to their previous question?

_____

_____

_____

SET 3

1. Two clients are arguing:

   Sally: "I don't think we should spend that much money."

   Sue: "But we want a nice trip."

   Sally: "Right, but we don't want to make ourselves sick thinking about money every day."

   Sue: "You're going to Australia once in your life, Sally!"

   What is your position here, to leave or intervene? Formulate what you might say to these clients.

   _____

   _____

   _____

   _____

   _____

   _____

   _____

   _____

   _____

9

CLOSING THE SALE

KEY TERM
Opinion

Closing the sale is the fifth and final step in the sales transaction. There are two parts to it: booking the space with the supplier/operator *and* getting the client's money. Before either of these can be accomplished, however, the client must first commit to taking the trip. Often, before doing this clients will first ask if you think it's the right trip for them, or will ask you to choose for them between two or more trips. This places the agent in a delicate position and makes it necessary to proceed with care.

 Customer: "Which of these resorts would *you* go to?"

 You will be asked that question plenty of times. How to answer? Should you give your opinion? In essence, travelers are asking you to choose a product or destination for them. But remember that you are not the one taking the trip, so get out of the client's dream. You can't choose for *someone else* what *you* like. It's all right to give your opinion, as long as you qualify it in one of two ways:

 1. *Back up the opinion with facts.* "I wouldn't go to that place because the CDC says there is an outbreak of polio. That makes me *personally* anxious. How do you feel about the situation?"
 2. *Explain why you hold the opinion.* "I would go to that place because it offers

the exciting nightlife that I crave on my trips. The other place is not as lively. Do you want nightlife as part of your vacation?" Similarly, when a client asks for your recommendation about a product, or wants you to help choose between two or more products, always back up your recommendations with facts. "I recommend this tour company because they have been carrying passengers for five years without an incident. I've had many customers use them and like them." Or phrase your answer within the context of what has been discussed. "Based on what you've told me, I would recommend this tour company."

Never tell customers that they will love a place or that it's perfect for them. You can't know that. Instead, find out if your customer agrees with your opinion and/or recommendation. The easiest way to do this is by asking a question, as we did in the example above.

ASKING FOR THE BOOKING

When you reach the point where you have nothing else to say or to explain, ask your client if there are any final questions. Here are two ways of doing it:

1. What are your questions?
2. What else would you like to know?

If there are any questions, clear these up. Then proceed directly and quickly to ask for the booking. If more than one person is involved, zero in on the decision maker, but be sure to include with a glance all members of the party.

There are three ways, discussed below, you can consider asking for the close. Which one to use depends on the individual you've been dealing with.

1. The first way is: "Would you like to book it?" This direct question succeeds in producing a "yes" when the client is a decisive person, as evidenced by the answers given throughout the conversation, such as, "I want . . . I need . . . I like . . . three days is entirely too short a time for us on a cruise; we don't begin to unwind; we want a seven-day trip." These people like to make their own decisions. So let them.

2. The second statement you can use is: "Let's book it, now." This suggests camaraderie. It helps the buyer who has difficulty making a choice. A client who has answered your questions with, "I don't know. . . I do like it, but I just can't decide right now. . . maybe I should think about it some more," may need a friendly, arm-around-the-shoulder nudging to make a decision. Be a buddy; do it together.

3. The third approach is to say: "I'm going to book it for you." Use this assertive statement with the customer who has shown signs of being incapable of making decisions. Reponses to you have been, "I've always wanted to but . . . sounds ideal

for me but what if . . . ." This person is ready to go, wants to go, but has trouble making an illusory dream a concrete happening. So you do it.

This third kind of traveler may panic at the definitiveness of the booking. A solution is to select only those packages that allow cancellation without penalty if they change their mind. Most of these people, though, will not cancel once the booking is made.

(*Hint:* If a client needs a final nudge to commit, try using a travel video to show what the vacation will be like.)

INVOLVING THE SUPPLIER IN THE CLOSING

Once you get a "yes" from the clients, turn immediately to your computer or call the supplier on the telephone. And book the trip while the clients are there, if at all possible. Hearing their trip confirmed gives clients a greater sense of commitment and lessens the chance that they will change their minds about taking the trip. It also reassures them that the details of their vacation are being properly looked after.

When you get through to the supplier, identify yourself with your first name and location. Then state your purpose in calling, and right away give the supplier the specifics for the booking. Don't waste time by making the supplier drag them out of you.

> Counsellor: "This is Linda from Magical Travel in Atlanta. I'd like to book two people to Mexico City on tour #202 departing September 4, using the Marie Isabel Sheraton Hotel, four nights."

> Counsellor: "I'd like to book . . . on the *Song of Norway,* June 10, category 4, preferring cabin 120 or similar with twin beds, for two adults."

What happens if you're foiled because the operator's lines are busy? What can you do to keep interest alive?

If the lines are busy, lag time is created. This gives clients time to get anxious, to reconsider, or to put the booking off until later. Use this lag time to advantage.

> Counsellor: "This tour company's lines are always busy; their programs are very popular."

> Counsellor: "This company's tours sell out every season; I hope I can get through soon."

One of the customers usually responds with something along the lines of, "Keep on trying. We hope we're not too late with our decision. . . ."

What happens when you get the supplier on the phone but the space you wanted to book is not available? You are always better off accepting alternative space and changing later if necessary than waffling or saying that you'll need to check with the client and you'll call back. Even the alternate space may not be available later.

If the client signals you to wait before accepting an alternative, you have a choice of actions at this point. If the client has been decisive throughout the sale, then it's okay to cover the phone (don't put the supplier on hold), briefly explain the alternative(s), and ask for an immediate answer. However, if the client has been indecisive about the trip or chatters a lot, motion "just a moment," but don't let the client intervene. Take charge and book the alternate. Afterwards, explain to your client what transpired. Say it's better to accept the alternative; it can be changed; that it's better than calling later and finding nothing available.

COLLECTING THE CLIENT'S MONEY

Now that the trip has been booked, it's time to move to part two of closing the sale: getting the client's money. Very often, though, buyers will profess not to have checkbook or credit cards with them, so they cannot put down the deposit today.

This is often a case of customers not wanting to part with their money until they absolutely have to. Or they may not be convinced that you really need the money now. You don't want a customer to leave without paying you. Paying is a powerful form of commitment. So a customer who doesn't pay may lose some commitment to you and the trip. Enthusiasm for the trip may be lost. Clients may become involved with other matters and forget to pay. Therefore, you must *ask* for the money in no uncertain terms!

Be definite. Make no apologies. A client who wants the trip must buy it. Say, "The deposit is $150 per person payable *now* to hold the confirmation. Will you pay with check or credit card?"

Do not say they *must* pay $150 per person. They don't *have* to do anything. And don't ask if it's all right to pay or whether they can handle the $150. If you've gotten this far, your client certainly understands the rules.

If you can't get all of the money now, at least try to get some, with an agreement to get the rest at a specific date. There will be times, however, when you won't be able to collect anything. If the client does not put money down, make use of the option time that the supplier gave you. Let your client know how many days there are in which to make payment, and that you will be in contact before the deadline.

Be sure that the client leaves feeling very committed to taking the trip, even though no deposit has been made. Ask such questions as,

> "I need to know if this is the trip you want."

> "Are the dates good for you?"

> "I will hold this tour for you. When can you bring the deposit?"

> "Space on this tour is almost sold out. I can hold your seats for just a few days."

Be sure to contact your client just before the option deadline, as you promised you would. Revive the enthusiasm and interest for the trip, and make sure that the money is being sent. Many times, clients will forget. If that option goes by, and the operator has received no money, the booking is cancelled.

If you let your clients know that you are willing to work with them, you have a better chance that they will remain committed and that you will close the sale.

EXPLAINING WHAT HAPPENS NEXT

A great source of client unrest and discontent is the uncertainty about what happens after the money has been paid, but before the actual departure on the trip—often a period of weeks or months. This uncertainty can be avoided if, at the time of closing, the counsellor simply takes a few minutes to explain to the client what happens next.

Counsellor: "I'll forward your money on to the tour company. When I receive confirmation from them, I will forward a copy of it to you. They will send us all your documents about ten days before your departure. I'll call you when they come in."

Without this advance menu of events—and your follow-up as promised, e.g., forwarding the confirmation—to put your clients at ease, all kinds of doubts and misgivings can arise. Did you forward their money? Why haven't they received confirmation? Is the tour company still in operation? You can spare your clients doubts (and the time it takes to answer their phone calls) by explaining what will happen next and when it will happen.

SAYING GOODBYE

Once the sale is done, don't jeopardize it by continuing the discussion. Say goodbye. This is a simple, yet often overlooked matter. It is your responsibility to initiate the client's departure.

As you make your final remarks, don't lean forward. That posture, remember, invites involvement and conversation. At this point, you want the transaction concluded. So sit up straight. Collect any scattered papers and brochures you've been working with. If you haven't already done so, give clients their brochure.

Then stand up. When the client stands up, it is all right, but not necessary, to shake hands goodbye. Clients who don't then move toward the door may not be able to handle this kind of situation well, and need help. Guide them to the door. Make small talk if necessary. Say anything you like about packing, the drive to the airport, or which kennel they're using for the dog. It is not advisable, however, to talk about the booking.

REVIEW

1. What two things must you do to "close a sale"?

_____

_____

_____

2. What three different phrases can you use to ask a client to book?

_____

_____

_____

3. When asking a client for money, you should

_____ a. be gentle; no one likes to part with money

_____ b. be definite and specific

_____ c. be apologetic; asking for money is an awful thing to do

4. The space you want to confirm with a supplier is not available. Should you

_____ a. tell the clients they can't go

_____ b. hang up, discuss alternatives with clients, and tell them to go home and think about the choices

_____ c. book an alternative, then discuss it with the clients

115

SET 2

1. Differentiate between the types of persons who respond best to each of the three ways to ask for a booking.

   _____

   _____

   _____

2. How should you substantiate your opinion?

   _____

   _____

3. Often, clients find that the time between giving you their money and going on the trip is one of uncertainty and suspicion. How can you ease their anxiety?

   _____

   _____

   _____

   _____

4. The clients who have been in your office for the last hour talk incessantly. However, you know how to control the conversation, and you have sold them a vacation. Now it's time to conclude the session. Demonstrate and describe your goodbye procedure.

   _____

   _____

   _____

   _____

_____

_____

_____

SET 3

1. Client: "Hello. We'd like to go on this ship [hands you the brochure]. What's your opinion of it?" Formulate a response.

_____

_____

_____

_____

_____

2. You've just booked a tour. You ask for the $100 deposit. The client says, "I won't have the money till the end of the month. Is that okay?" Formulate a response.

_____

_____

_____

_____

_____

3. The client calls and says, "We're supposed to leave on our trip in just three weeks and we haven't received anything yet. What's the problem?" How could this client's frustration have been avoided?

_____

_____

_____

_____

_____

_____

10

SELLING PACKAGE LAND TOURS

Three-fourths of Americans who take international trips book their overseas vacation through a travel agent. These trips can be any of various types: educational, adventure, sporting, cultural, average sightseeing, "meet the people," rest and relaxation, to say "I've been there," or romantic.

- 22.8 percent of the Americans on trips to overseas destinations use a pre-paid package or inclusive tour.

- 67.8 percent of U.S. outbound travelers spend more than one week in overseas destinations.

- Only 32.5 percent of Americans traveling overseas visit more than one country on their trip abroad.

- Over 65 percent of U.S. outbound travelers have taken at least five previous overseas trips in their lifetime.

Knowing these statistics will guide you in suggesting international vacations, in planning itineraries, and in selecting products.

Depending on their background and/or experience, travelers may define "tour" in several ways. To some it means a group of people doing the same things at the same time over a specified period. To others, it means visiting a foreign place and "checking it out." Many people wrinkle their noses and say they wouldn't be caught dead on a tour because their definition of a tour is a form of travel only for old people.

In fact, however, a tour is not as narrow as any of these travelers define it. Indeed, a wide variety of tours are available, and in almost all cases either you can find one that matches up with what your clients want, or you can plan a personalized tour for them.

A tour is a prearranged and at least partially prepaid trip offered by a tour company. It also can be a personalized trip (foreign independent travel) arranged for clients by the counsellor, with or without the involvement of a tour company.

EXPLAINING TYPES OF TOURS

The tour may be escorted, hosted, independent (often called a city package), fly/drive, foreign independent travel, or charter. Listed below are the various types, and suggestions for qualifying which clients may be suitable for which type of tour.

ESCORTED TRIPS

An escorted trip is rigidly structured, with a continuous sequence of daily events closely directed hour by hour by an escort and a tour guide.

The tour escort is responsible for the passengers and their belongings. This is the person who makes sure that they are safe and comfortable and that their needs are being met, that all the passengers stay together, and that they are all where they are supposed to be at all times, whether at a museum, on the bus, or in the dining room.

The tour guide, on the other hand, is responsible for giving sightseeing information to the passengers. The guide tells them where they are, what they are looking at, and why. Both the escort and the guide are an integral part of the success of an escorted vacation.

The advantages of an escorted trip are:

1. *Camaraderie.* Because they travel together for a period of time, the passengers form friendships, enjoy companionship for a while, and share experiences.

2. *Upfront costs.* Because most or all of an escorted tour's costs are prepaid, passengers know what to expect financially.

3. *Ease of travel.* Escorted tour companies plan all events, provide an air-conditioned or heated motorcoach, and buy any needed transportation tickets.

4. *Safety and security.* Tours offer greater safety and security because the escorts and guides know the area and the local customs; they know what procedures to take in case of a mishap. Good tour companies will even have their escorts carry emergency funds should they be needed by the group.

5. *Onsite travel discourse.* The tour guide's job is to be an interesting talking guidebook. This not only saves the passenger from having to do advance reading, but also brings the destination alive and makes it memorable.

Escorted trips are ideal for those travelers who like togetherness, supervision, and knowing exactly what they will be doing and when they will be doing it. These can be people of any age, income, or travel experience. Be aware, however, that too often both agents and clients make the mistake of assuming that because travelers are of a certain age (i.e., over sixty-five), or have never visited a particular country before, or don't know the language, an escorted tour automatically qualifies as the best trip for them. This isn't true. Travelers of any age or experience may object to the high degree of regimentation. Therefore, if clients say they want to go on an escorted tour, first make sure that they know what an escorted tour is like.

HOSTED TRIPS

A hosted trip provides accommodations, airport transfers, at least one half-day sightseeing tour in each city or area regardless of whether the stay is for one day or two weeks, and a *host* in each city. Unlike the escorted trip, there are no other planned events; there is an abundance of free time for the travelers to use as they wish. The host represents the tour company and is on duty at specified times each day at the hotel to provide advice, recommendations, help, and directions. As at a party, the host comes by every so often to be sure the guests are having a good time and that they have enough to eat and drink, but does not escort the travelers anywhere.

The advantages of a hosted trip are:

1. *Security.* The major items of the trip are preplanned, prebooked, and prepaid. Your clients know they have a place to stay in each city and they know how they will get from city to city. And they have the comfort of having someone to turn to if they need help.

2. *Flexibility.* Passengers have plenty of free time to do what they want when they want.

3. *Guidance.* The host is there to tell them how to rent a car for the day, how to get to the museum, and where to go for good local food.

4. *Independence.* Other than a three- or four-hour sightseeing excursion in each place, travelers are on their own and use their time any way they wish.

Hosted vacations are a good choice for those clients who want some direction, such as where they stay and how to get there, but otherwise want to be free to make their own choices.

INDEPENDENT TOURS

An independent tour (often described as "barebones") has two defining features: 1) it always includes accommodations, and 2) travelers are completely on their own, i.e., there is no escort or host. Any other components, such as air, transfers, taxes, or sightseeing excursions, may be included depending on the tour company's offerings, or added on at extra cost at the time of booking the barebones package or at the destination. Travelers on an independent tour have a great degree of flexibility, choice, and independence. A barebones tour is attractive to independent travelers not because of the freedom it offers, but because of the inexpensive upfront cost. However, these travelers often are disillusioned because they end up paying more out-of-pocket costs for items that could have been purchased at better prices if they were part of the package. For travelers who are interested in an independent tour, make sure that a barebones really is a deal. For example, will your clients really go to Rome and *not* tour the Vatican? If the answer is "no," then sell them a tour that *includes* a visit to the Vatican. The total package cost will be higher (because more is included) but the clients get the essentials at less cost (because the tour company purchases them in bulk in advance and passes the savings on to clients who book in advance).

If, indeed, the package is suitable for the clients, suggest that they do some advance reading, because they will be taking care of all matters themselves, and it will be up to them to fill in large amounts of unscheduled time.

FLY/DRIVE TOURS

A fly/drive tour—self-planned touring around a country by rental car or train— uses accommodations selected from the tour company's participants list. The transportation and the hotels are listed in the brochure for one price. There is usually a selection of prices based on the type of car the clients choose, the length of the trip, and how many hotel nights they want prepaid. Some accommodations may be prearranged and paid for prior to arrival, with the balance of hotel stays booked and paid for en route. On other fly/drive programs travelers simply pay for the number of hotel nights they want but book them along the way. Regardless of the accommodations plan, the fly/drive tour company will supply your clients with maps, itinerary suggestions, and a list of participating hotels/inns.

Those who enjoy fly/drive view the following as benefits:

1. *Freedom of movement.* Fly/drive offers travelers great freedom of movement because they do not stay in one city or place. They can choose a route at a whim's notice. Yet there may be one hundred hotels in the vicinity that will accept their vouchers (prepaid coupons). Depending upon the program they have purchased, they can have one hotel phone ahead to the next for reservations, or the travelers may simply arrive unannounced.

2. *Independence.* Travelers plot their own route. All sightseeing is on their own— no group tours whatsoever.

3. *Challenge.* Travelers depend on themselves. They are forced to participate more in the local customs and to meet the people. They do the driving; they read the signs; they find their own way. They create their own sightseeing route.

Advise fly/drive clients about the road conditions and the rules for driving in foreign countries. Tell them what the speed limits are, if any. Tell them about predictable habits of the local drivers. Suggest that they learn the international driving symbols. These fly/drive people need to be able to take care of themselves. And they need to be able to deal comfortably with local customs and situations. If they seem to need more items taken care of, you might suggest an escorted trip instead. If they seem nervous on their own, yet they don't want group travel, you might suggest a chauffeur-driven car tour.

FOREIGN INDEPENDENT TRAVEL (FIT)

An FIT is a customized, detailed, preplanned day-by-day itinerary for individual travelers. Organizing such a highly independent tour will call upon all of your skills, knowledge, resources, imagination, and creativity. The FIT components can include any or all such items as the following: air transportation, local transportation such as car rental, ferries, trains, buses, hotels, meals, and entertainment tickets. Your clients may request that their daily itinerary be completely planned, booked, and prepaid in advance, down to the very last detail. Or they can request a basic itinerary and fill in the options themselves as they go along. The details are dependent entirely on the clients' preferences. Either way, the result is a planned daily sequence of events with the travelers acting as their own tour escort and using the FIT itinerary as the tour guide.

Travelers who use an FIT consider the following as advantages:

1. *Total freedom of choice.* The FIT allows the clients choices of doing what they want when they want, as opposed to a group tour that requires passengers to be in Rome on day three.

2. *The thrill of exploration.* Travelers can build into their vacation any personal interests or lengthy investigations in an area. They have only themselves to please, so if they want to spend seven days at the Louvre in Paris, it's all right.

3. *Financial control.* Travelers regulate the costs by the choices they make. They can spend $20 a night to stay at a local inn and spend $125 for a dinner at a castle, or they can stay at the castle for $125 a night and eat at the inn for $20.

4. *Closer local contact.* Because there is no tour company escort or local guide, clients have to deal with the local people in order to get around. They might even learn some of the country's language!

5. *Variety.* FIT planning provides an optional assortment of touring methods and means: a rental car one day, the train the next day, a ferryboat the next, or a train throughout.

6. *Knowledge.* Because travelers using an FIT participate in its formation, they must first read about and study their destination.

People who are suited for an FIT like to wander around on their own, and *are capable of doing so.* Roaming around may seem attractive to many more of your clients than really are suited for successfully carrying out such an independent vacation. Remind them that being their own group leader makes them responsible for their time, whereabouts, safety, schedules, needs, and having their expectations met.

CHARTER TOURS

A charter tour is an inexpensive air/land trip designed to transport and accommodate a planeload of passengers (often as many as two hundred fifty or more at a time). A charter tour includes air, airport/hotel transfers, accommodations, and maybe a sightseeing trip of a few hours, all packaged for one price. All participants agree to leave on the assigned day and time and all return at an assigned time. They agree to the accommodations, whatever they are. The tour participants sign a form, called a waiver, at the time of booking, stating that they understand that the operator has the right to change what is necessary in order to keep the costs low. The hotel may be advertised as the Smith House, but at the last minute it may be changed to Billie Bob's Hut. The departure date may be changed from Wednesday to Thursday. The participants agree to the tour as is and as it needs to be changed, and in return get a low price.

Most charter operators use aircraft designed to carry as many people as possible, which leaves less space per passenger for comfort. Additionally, these operators generally assume few responsibilities. They do no counselling. They simply take your client's reservations. The less work and fewer services they have to provide agents and passengers, the cheaper they can operate the charter.

Charters offer three main advantages:

1. *Low price.*

2. *Simple selection.* The very nature of a charter means that neither you nor your clients need to weigh choices or make comparisons. Clients either buy as is or they don't buy it.

3. *Plenty of free time.*

Most clients who consider using a charter tour simply want to get away, and they don't want to spend much money doing it. Stress to these travelers, however, that they can't be picky about the arrangements, and that they may have to adapt quickly to changes in plans. Remind them that they have to sign a waiver agreeing to any changes.

DIFFERENTIATING PRICE LEVELS OF TOURS

There are three price levels in any form of organized travel (except charter): deluxe, first-class, and budget. Deluxe is top-of-the-line, first-class, despite its name, is really middle-class, and budget is what its name implies. All three do a good job *within their own category*. It is important for your clients to understand what they will receive in exchange for each price. Don't let them pick a tour or select an itinerary by price alone. Consider some of the following factors that make people happy on a tour.

On the deluxe level the hotels are the finest available. If the tour is in major cities, the hotels are centrally located. They have the comfort the price commands. If meals are included, the deluxe programs have the most meals and the best menu selections. If the program is escorted, the deluxe level provides the best. Sightseeing is explicit and includes all entrance fees. Group size is usually limited to a maximum of twenty-eight people who expect to be treated to the best service, care, and attention.

The first-class price level uses the middle category of hotels (and often they are not as centrally located), packs more people onto a motorcoach per departure, and has more departures. The sightseeing itinerary has longer stretches on the bus or train and less time spent at actual sightseeing locations. Fewer meals are included, so travelers must carry extra funds for meals. On the other hand, there is greater freedom to eat where people, individually, want.

The budget price level uses budget or standard accommodations, often outside cities, includes even fewer meals or less variety in the food, crowds even more people on the motorcoaches, and does more sightseeing from the windows of the bus as opposed to actually visiting the places. There are usually more optionals to buy as opposed to already included.

DISCUSSING ITINERARIES

Hosted, independent, fly/drive, and charter tours have few, if any, scheduled events. Escorted and FIT tours, on the other hand, usually have a great many. Thoroughly covering the selected itinerary of events will let your clients know exactly what they'll be getting and, if done efficiently and enthusiastically, will help close the sale. Here are some tips for making the best presentation possible.

Gear the pace of your presentation to the type of trip. Some itineraries are leisurely and some are rushed. Some people want to see and do as much as they can in the allotted time, while others want to have time to proceed more unhurriedly. Therefore, when discussing a 10-country tour in an 8-day itinerary that is full of action, speak faster than usual. Pause only *before* you say something exciting ("On day two . . ." [pause]) or to make sure that your audience is still with you.

However, when discussing an itinerary for travelers who need a chance to digest the information, or for those who are interested in buying a more slowly-paced trip, pause to distinguish important points and to give the correct impression that the trip *does* proceed more slowly.

Start with the "Day-By-Day" account in the brochure. For instance, the itinerary says:

> **Day 1 Stockholm to Oslo, Norway**
> An early breakfast and then we depart by train to Norway. A relaxing day watching the passing scenes of Sweden's lakes and forests. Arriving in Oslo in mid-afternoon, there is time to explore this unique city, nestled at the tip of a 60-mile fjord. (B)

Do not read. That takes too long and clients generally feel that they can read just as well as you can.

Start with Day 1 and summarize each day. This is what you might say to summarize this day:

> Counsellor: "Breakfast is included this morning. Then you go by train across Sweden to Oslo. You arrive mid-afternoon and have the rest of the day free." (*Note:* If the Swedish scenery or Oslo is important to these customers, it is all right to elaborate. Otherwise, proceed to Day 2.)

Keep pen or marker in hand, and use it to circle, point, and underline what interests them. For instance, if they want to be sure that the tour overnights in Oslo, circle Oslo on the itinerary to reinforce the fact that you are giving them what they want.

Use the route map provided for the itinerary. After you have summarized Day 1, Sweden to Oslo by train, trace that part of the route on the map. Your customers' eyes should follow your tracing. This technique helps keep customers focused on the itinerary and lessens the chance that they will jump ahead to price. Continue on to each consecutive day. Show the continuation of the route on the map.

Note free time vs. traveling time vs. sightseeing time. The balance among these could be the deciding factor in whether or not the clients like the itinerary, and it should be carefully noted.

PRESENTING ITINERARY FEATURES AND BENEFITS

After the day-by-day account has been covered, talk about the "features" included in the tour. Sample:

- Escorted from arrival in Paris
- Airport transfers in Paris
- Twin-bedded rooms with private shower in first-class hotels
- 11 breakfasts, 9 lunches, 7 dinners
- Farewell dinner party
- Air-conditioned motorcoach
- Sightseeing excursions as listed in day-by-day itinerary
- Evening champagne cruise on the Seine
- All local taxes
- Handling and tips for one piece of luggage per person

Ile de la Cité, Paris
Photo: Courtesy Air France

Note to your customers the following details about the features.

Meals. Say how many meals are included and mention any special affairs or dinner parties.

Hotels. Mention where the hotels are located and whether they are in the cities or on the outskirts. Discuss the kind of hotels they are, whether simple or elaborate, charming or utilitarian. Are any of them landmarks, well-known properties, or otherwise special? In brochures of escorted tours, you can often find such information in the front section. If not, or you want more, go to the *Official Hotel & Resort Guide.*

Special arrangements. Note anything extraordinary about the sightseeing tours, such as the evening champagne cruise on the Seine.

Next point out the benefits of the various features. Stress those features you know to be important to the clients. Let's say, for example, using the features on the Paris tour, that the clients are concerned about the accommodations and food because Paris is so expensive.

> Counsellor: "Your room will have a private shower. Hotel rooms with private shower are expensive when not purchased as part of a package so you save

money this way. Even the taxes are included so you needn't worry about paying more upon check-out. Most of your meals are included so you won't have to spend a lot of time in busy Paris looking for restaurants with reasonable prices."

Always discuss the itinerary and the features and benefits of a tour before discussing price. You will have a better chance of eliminating an objection to what the tour costs, assuming you've selected a tour in the customer's price range to begin with.

DETERMINING PRICE

As a general rule, charters and escorted trips carry flat, inflexible rates. However, independent, hosted, and fly/drive tours have variable price structures depending upon the price level of the trip and the options available within those levels. These options are usually displayed in the second section of the brochure.

Because each page of the brochure is filled with numbers, it tends to be confusing to most customers. To alleviate the complexity, it is best that you handle the brochure. Let's say that your customers want a hosted tour in Mexico City and Acapulco. The following conversation is picked up at the point that you are discussing price options, using the sample page below.

> Counsellor: "The price for this package depends on the hotels selected. Let's take a look in the deluxe category at the combination of the Camino Real in Mexico City and the Acapulco Princess in Acapulco. Rates range from $609 to $815 per person depending on the type of room you prefer."

Point this out in the brochure; have them follow your pen as you map out the procedure. Find the two hotels listed at the bottom of the page and read across; locate the TWIN column and read down; where the two pieces of information meet is the price.

UNDERSTANDING THE USE OF IT NUMBERS

Every package tour has an identification code called the Inclusive Tour (IT or I.T.) number that is assigned by the tour operator. You will need to use this number to identify to the tour operator which tour your clients are interested in or want to book. The IT number either will be printed with each tour itinerary, or the brochure may list all ITs on a single page.

Refer to the sample page on page 130 for the Mexican Sun-Brero hosted tour. The IT number is IT8CO1FH06. The IT stands for inclusive tour; the CO is the

MEXICAN SUN-BRERO: MEXICO CITY (3 NIGHTS) • ACAPULCO (4 NIGHTS)-IT8CO1FH06

LAND RATES PER PERSON (Tax Included) – European Plan

MEXICO CITY	ACAPULCO	CATEGORY	EFFECTIVE DATES	TWIN	MEXICAN TRIPLE	SINGLE
PALACIO REAL	AUTO RITZ	(ROH)	1/03-4/19	169	139	249
	ACAPULCO DOLPHINS	(ROH)	1/02-27	175	149	285
			1/28-4/02	205	165	339
			4/03-30	169	145	269
CALINDA GENEVE OR EL PRESIDENTE CHAPULTEPEC·	ACAPULCO MARIS	(ROH)	1/02-25	215	169	369
			1/26-4/01	249	189	435
			4/02-30	209	165	359
	COPACABANA	(OCEANVIEW)	1/03-22, 3/19-4/09	249	200	439
			1/23-3/18	279	220	499
	CALINDA	(MOUNTAINVIEW)	1/03-31	295	230	529
			2/01-4/09	309	240	559
		(OCEANVIEW)	1/03-31	309	240	559
			2/01-4/09	329	250	589
	RADISSON PARAISO	(ROH)	1/03-30	265	219	465
			1/31-3/15	295	239	529
			3/16-4/10	255	215	445
	ACAPULCO RITZ	(SUPERIOR)	1/03-4/19	295	239	515
KRYSTAL ROSA WESTIN GALERIA PLAZA OR CROWNE PLAZA··	HYATT CONTINENTAL	(LANAI)	1/03-17	309	NA	555
			1/18-31. 3/01-4/16	339	NA	619
			2/01-29	355	NA	649
		(OCEANVIEW)	1/03-17	339	279	619
			1/18-31. 3/01-4/16	385	309	709
			2/01-29	405	325	745
	ACAPULCO PLAZA	(TOWER)	1/03-17	339	275	609
			1/18-4/16	399	325	739
		(SUITE)	1/03-4/16	459	365	855
	HYATT REGENCY	(MOUNTAINVIEW)	1/03-17	339	NA	615
			1/18-31. 3/01-4/16	385	NA	705
			2/01-29	399	NA	739
		(OCEANVIEW)	1/03-17	369	305	675
			1/18-31. 3/01-4/16	429	345	799
			2/01-29	449	355	829
MARIA ISABEL SHERATON OR WESTIN CAMINO REAL	PIERRE MARQUES (MAP)	(STANDARD)	1/03-4/08	609	540	1015
		(SUPERIOR)		675	585	1155
		(DELUXE)		745	635	1289
		(JR. SUITE)		789	665	1379
	ACAPULCO PRINCESS (MAP)	(STANDARD)	1/03-4/08	609	540	1015
		(SUPERIOR)		675	585	1155
		(DELUXE)		745	635	1289
		(JR. SUITE)		815	679	1429

Courtesy of Friendly Holidays Inc. Reprinted by permission.

airline code (Continental); the FH is Friendly Holidays. The other numbers are individually assigned by the tour operator as part of their filing system.

Another reason for using the IT number is to claim override commission (extra earnings above the basic commission offered by the tour company) on your clients' international air tickets. In order for you to claim an override commission on the air fare, the tour must be booked and prepaid, *and* the tour's IT number must be reflected on the clients' airline tickets in the "tour code box." For example, if the standard airline commission on an international ticket is eight percent, you could get an extra three percent. Be sure to write 11 in the "commission box," not 8 + 3. Be aware that if you claim eleven percent air commission and fail to list the IT number, or list it improperly, the Airlines Reporting Corporation (ARC) will send your agency a debit memo demanding the return of the extra three percent commission you kept.

CLAIMING COMMISSION ON FIT TOURS

When doing FITs, you are booking pieces of a trip with several different suppliers/ operators. Some pieces may have an IT number, such as an American Express three-day city package in London. Other pieces of the trip may not, such as a one-night's hotel in Frankfurt. As long as one piece of the land trip bears an IT number, you may claim the eleven percent commission on the airline ticket. If the FIT has more than one segment with an IT number, simply choose one of the numbers to put on the ticket.

CLAIMING COMMISSION ON FITs THAT HAVE NO IT NUMBERS

Many times you will build a personalized itinerary with no segments having an IT number. You can still claim override commission, however, if your company is a member of the American Society of Travel Agents' operator's division. ASTA assigns its own IT numbers, which can be used by the members of this division. The numbers are recognized by the airlines. Call or write ASTA for further information.

PAYING THE SUPPLIERS

After your clients pay their required deposit amount, you in turn pay your deposit to the supplier/operator via agency check or Miscellaneous Charges Order (MCO). If you pay by check, you usually can't deduct commission. If you pay by MCO, however, you may claim commission. If you pay by MCO, make sure first that the operator accepts this form of payment.

The advantages for a company to accept an airline form are:

1. They receive more bookings because travel agencies like to use the forms.

2. There is a better guarantee that the payment is good, as opposed to checks that can bounce.

There is also a disadvantage:

1. Payment is delayed because it goes to the ARC before it is distributed to the operator.

If you send in an MCO without checking beforehand to see if the company will accept it, you run the risk that reservations may be cancelled because proper payment was not received on time, or that documents will be delayed because proper procedures were not followed.

When you make the final payment (less deposit) to the operator, you may pay by agency check, MCO, or Tour Order, provided the operator accepts the form of payment. Note that you can use a Tour Order when paying in full or making a final payment on tours, but you can't use it to make tour deposits.

Keep track of when you are supposed to receive all the tour documents from the operator. If you do not get them at the anticipated time, call immediately.

When you do receive them, go over all the vouchers, tickets, and coupons to be sure that everything that has been paid for is included and accounted for. Only after you've checked everything should you call your clients to advise them that the documents have arrived at your office. (*Note:* Be sure to go over each voucher with your clients.)

REVIEW

SET 1

1. What is an escorted tour? _____

_____

2. Why would someone choose a charter tour? _____

_____

3. Why is it important to record the IT number on the airline ticket? _____

_____

_____

4. What three price levels do organized tours offer?

_____

_____

_____

5. What is the difference between a tour escort and tour guide?

_____

6. An independent tour is also called

_____ and _____.

SET 2

1. What are some of the advantages of an escorted tour?

_____

_____

_____

_____

2. When do you discuss prices for an independent tour? For an escorted tour?

_____

_____

_____

_____

3. Give a general description of people who prefer Foreign Independent Travel.

_____

_____

_____

_____

4. In what order do you discuss the information on the pages of a brochure describing an escorted tour?

_____

_____

_____

_____

SET 3

1. Clients (in their late forties): "We want to visit Spain and Portugal. We've never been anywhere in Europe before, so we thought we better go on an escorted

tour. Can you show us some kind of package?" How should you proceed with this request?

_____

_____

_____

_____

_____

_____

_____

_____

2. What words can you look for in an itinerary to help you determine the amount of free time versus traveling time versus sightseeing time?

Free time: _____

_____

Traveling time: _____

_____

Sightseeing time: _____

_____

3. What is the value of gearing the pace of your discussion about a trip to the pace of the itinerary of the trip that you're presenting?

_____

_____

_____

_____

_____

_____

_____

_____

_____

_____

4. Turn this feature into a benefit: hotel with full American breakfast.

_____

_____

_____

_____

_____

11

SELLING CRUISES

KEY TERMS
Guarantees
Supersavers

Cruising is not just for the old and/or the wealthy. Single people, senior citizens, families, honeymooners, couples, high school groups, and the local bridge club go on cruises. Firefighters, teachers, salespersons, CEOs of major corporations, secretaries, and electricians go on cruises. To satisfy this wide variety of cruisers, some ships have a party atmosphere; others have a more reserved atmosphere. Some ships are richly appointed, while others are splashy and colorful. Some ships are large enough to carry over 2,600 passengers and 750 crew members, while others are small enough to provide an intimate atmosphere for as few as fifty passengers. It is the counsellor's responsibility to know enough about the different cruise lines and ships in order to put the right person on the right cruise.

ADVANTAGES OF CRUISING

A cruise is a popular vacation option because it is a self-contained floating resort that offers a wide variety of onboard activities as well as travel to different places. It has a number of advantages which you should use as selling points.

1. *Predictable expenses.* Clients pay one upfront price that usually includes ship transportation, ship accommodations, all meals, airport/dock transfers, entertainment on board, taxes, and quite often, the round-trip air fare between hometown and port of embarkation. Therefore, the only items clients need to budget for are drinks, tips, and personal purchases (including gambling money, souvenirs, medical services, and beauty parlor services).

2. *Travel convenience.* Cruise vacationers travel in total comfort without having to figure out the route or worry about finding a gas station. They don't have to get up at dawn to be on the tour bus. They don't have to sit still in a motorcoach seat for hours while they travel to that next destination. And they pack and unpack their suitcases only once, yet visit several places.

3. *Range of experiences.* Cruises offer a wide variety of activities and experiences. Relaxation and excitement are easily attainable. The variety of activities is constant. There are opportunities to meet all kinds of people. Travelers in pursuit of glamour, prestige, or romance can find it on a cruise.

4. *Flexibility.* Cruisers can participate in everything offered or do nothing at all. Or they can sample a little of everything. Because they don't have to make prior arrangements, order tickets (except for shore excursions), or stand in line, they can change their minds at any time.

5. *Dining at no cost.* Cruise dining offers an array of foods to suit the most discriminating palates. It satisfies both the hot dog craver and the lobster lover. And no matter how often or how much they eat cruisers never have to pay for it because it has already been included in the prepaid price. They can have a full course meal in the dining room or a sandwich on deck. If they can't decide between steak and veal at dinner, they can order both—after all, it's paid for.

6. *Variety of destinations and sightseeing.* Because most cruises stop at a diversity of ports of call, travelers can experience different cultures, scenery, shopping, and activities, ranging from beach parties to historical excursions. Or they can pass up any or all of it by staying on the ship when it docks.

The advantages of cruising can be summed up by saying that it is financially attractive, comfortable, and offers different types of fun, and, therefore, is suitable for different types of people, singly or together.

DISCUSSING CRUISING IN GENERAL

What is wrong with this scenario?

Customers: "We'd like to go on a cruise. What do you suggest?"

Agent: "I suggest Roundabout Cruise Line's Caribbean ships which are very popular. Here's their brochure."

The major mistake is that the agent immediately matched the product before getting to know anything about the customers. The second mistake is that the agent assumed that Roundabout Cruises are good for everyone. The customers might respond that they have been on Roundabout and hated everything about the line. These clients will not trust anything else this agent recommends. If the prospects do not say whether or not they have been on a cruise before, ask them immediately.

This agent also assumed that cruising will satisfy the customers' wish for a vacation. People often think they want a particular type of vacation when in fact they have little or no idea what that type of trip is like and whether it can fulfill their expectations. Suppose all they want to do is lie by the water for days on end and get a suntan. Is cruising the vacation for them? Or should they be introduced instead to the idea of a beach vacation in the Bahamas Family Islands?

Finally, the agent limited the market by assuming that they probably want to cruise the Caribbean, on an ordinary cruise ship. People may know they want a cruise, but they don't necessarily know *where* they want to cruise because their knowledge of where cruises go is limited. Open up the possibilities of Alaska, the

Geiranger Fjord, Norway
Photo: Courtesy Norwegian National Travel Office

Mediterranean, Mexico, Hawaii, the Norwegian fjords, Tahiti, etc. Even if their response is something like "We just want to go to the Caribbean," you have introduced the idea of exploration in other parts of the world in the future.

In summary, first learn what your customers want in a vacation. Find out why they are going and what they expect to come back with. This is the only way you can determine that cruising is a choice that will fulfill their dreams and wishes. Once you've established that it is, then discuss the choices of appropriate ships that cruise in the area.

Every conversation with prospects will be different. They may say anything. But, as discussed before, there are general statements you can use to keep the conversation moving forward. Here is a sample:

Customers: "We're interested in going on a cruise. What do you suggest?"

Counsellor: "Have you been on a cruise before?"

Customers: "No, but we thought we'd like it for a change."

Counsellor: [picking up on the words "for a change"] "What type of vacation do you usually take?"

Customers: "Well, we've been going to Florida for the past six years. We still want a hot weather vacation with some time at the beach, but we want more of a variety of other things to do this time."

Counsellor: "What attracts you to cruising as the option?"

Customers: "I could gamble and play cards, and mother, here, could do more shopping. We both want to see a couple of new places, but we don't want to drive and we don't want to be on a tour bus all week. We're both big eaters and we understand that the food is unlimited! We've never been out of the States before, and we thought this would be a safe adventure for us."

The customers are giving you good information that will lead you to some safe conclusions: They know some things about cruising. They know why they want to cruise. They are not experienced international travelers. So far, it seems that cruising probably will satisfy what they are looking for.

Now talk about cruising in general. Be enthusiastic and use appropriate adjectives, such as exotic, sparkling, enticing, breezy, colorful, ancient, mysterious, exciting, delicious. Talk about the activities and the food first since your customers have indicated an interest in them. (Food and activities are two big selling points for most people.)

DISCUSSING MEALS

When you explain dining procedures to your customers you will need to tell them what meals are offered and how to select a sitting for the meals. Don't stop there, however. Let them know that dining aboard a cruise ship is an experience. Create enthusiasm for participating in these experiences by painting word pictures that depict the indulgent service, the richness and variety of the food, and the colorful dining atmosphere.

> Counsellor: "Food galore is standard on cruises. All ships offer breakfast, lunch, dinner, and late-night buffet. For breakfast, you have a choice of ordering it sent to your cabin, or eating a buffet out on deck, or going into the dining room and ordering off the menu . . . or you may do all three! And there is no charge no matter how much or how often you eat."

It is especially important to guide first-time cruisers in their choice of the meal sitting. Don't just ask them which sitting they want. How do they know? And be sure to point out that since their schedule aboard ship will be different from their schedule at home, it may affect the time they normally want to eat. For example, on the cruise, they won't have just come home from work when they go to dinner.

> Counsellor: "You must make a choice of meal sitting: first or late [or whatever terminology the cruise line uses]. You then eat in the dining room at those hours during the entire cruise. [In other words, this doesn't apply to on-deck buffets and room service.] First sitting hours are 7:00 A.M. for breakfast, noon for lunch, and 6:30 P.M. for dinner. Breakfast and lunch times can be altered by eating out on deck instead of in the dining room. So dinner time is the inflexible meal. Late sitting hours are 7:30 A.M. for breakfast, 1:30 P.M. for lunch, and 8:30 P.M. for dinner. Which sitting you choose is a matter of personal preference. Here are some common reasons for choosing one or the other. First sitting gives you more time after dinner for entertainment, dancing, and so forth, and a few more hours before the late-night buffet. But that also means less time before dinner for cocktails or a nap, and you may need to hurry back from the shore excursion to get ready for dinner. More families and seniors eat early. Late sitters have more time before dinner for cocktails or a nap. Dinner tends to be less hectic at the second sitting because the waiters do not have to serve another round of guests immediately afterward. By the time dinner is over, though, it's 10:00 P.M. or later. Which kind of schedule is more important to you?"

DISCUSSING ONBOARD ACTIVITIES

Onboard cruise activities are divided into two parts: daytime and evening. Both should be explained before you try to select a certain ship for the clients. Be specific. Don't just say, "There are so many things to do on a cruise." Take a few minutes to give examples so clients can visualize themselves doing these things.

Let them know that onboard daytime activities range from stretching out in a deck chair to working out in aerobics classes, from winning money at bingo and horseracing to spending money in the shopping arcade.

Tell them that onboard nighttime activities include floorshows, dancing, gambling, partying in one of the bars, the Captain's cocktail party, first-run movies, talent shows, and masquerade parades.

When discussing onboard activities, stress to customers that they aren't required to participate in anything. They have freedom of choice—which includes doing nothing at all. They will know what their choices are because a daily calendar of activities will be placed in their cabin each evening.

Be sure to point out those activities that are not included in the cruise price and for which extra money will be needed, such as drinks, shopping, shore excursions, gambling, and personal activities such as a massage or a beauty shop visit. This kind of information will help your clients to budget extra funds for the vacation.

DISCUSSING ONSHORE ACTIVITIES

The destinations are often a main reason that clients cruise. These clients will ask, "Should we take a ship's organized shore excursions, or is it feasible for us to sightsee on our own?" Only the clients themselves can ultimately answer that question, but you can guide them in several ways.

1. Describe the ports, talk about what there is to see and do in each, and make any distinctions among the ports.

2. Answer such questions as, "What kind of distances are involved?," "Can we walk to any of these things of interest?," "How expensive are the taxis?"

3. Get a shore excursion booklet from the cruise line that details the selections, times, and prices for the excursions in each port.

4. Let the clients know that the cruise director will give a talk about the ports of call before the ship docks at the first one. The talk will cover general information about the places, specific information about the planned excursions offered by the line, as well as tips on how passengers can get a group together themselves and hire a local guide or taxi, or sightsee on their own. Depending on the port, some clients may prefer just to sleep on the beach, play golf, go diving, or shop. Emphasize that the choice is theirs.

5. If they are interested in a destination-intensive cruise, however, such as a Nile River cruise, the excursions are usually included in the cruise price. Be sure that you mention this fact, and when you study particular cruise lines note whether this is the case. With such information in hand, the clients can better decide if they want to take the ship's shore excursions in none, one, any, or all of the ports. And they will be better prepared to have successful independent jaunts if that's what they want to do.

SELLING THE CABINS

Too often counsellors don't pay enough attention to cabin selection—and neither do clients. Counsellors often match their clients with a cabin solely on the basis of cost without considering other important factors. Clients, on the other hand, er-

roneously think that because they won't be spending much time in the cabin, careful selection isn't important. As a result, clients can end up with a cabin that is unsuitable in size and location. This can sour an otherwise wonderful vacation.

For this reason, it is important to advise clients about the variety of choices available and the pros and cons of each. In addition to price, discuss with them location—front to back, top to bottom, inside or outside—and type of bed arrangement (twin beds, double, queen, king, and berths, which are uppers and lowers).

Advise them, too, not to compare a cabin to their bedroom at home or to a hotel room. Cabins are usually smaller, often a great deal smaller, with a small private bathroom. If your travelers embark on a cruise thinking that their cabin will be like the suites they have seen on *Love Boat,* they will be greatly disappointed—unless, of course, they have purchased a suite. Most cabins are designed for two people, with little space left over. So if more than two passengers share the cabin, while some clients may say it's quite cozy, others will call it crowded.

In discussing location, be sure to cover the advantages and disadvantages of each factor. For example, the *inside* cabins are cheaper. But no natural light ever comes into the room. An advantage of this is that you can take a nap at any hour of the day because it will seem like night. Then again, when you wake up in the morning, the beautiful sky and sea cannot be viewed; the room is still pitch dark. You have to get dressed and go outside to see what the weather is like or whether you've arrived at port yet. Some people tend to feel claustrophobic in the inside rooms. Some lines have tried to alleviate that feeling by hanging curtains on the wall, even though there is no window.

The *outside* cabins tend to feel bigger because natural light comes into the room. You know when you arrive; you know what the weather is like. The room can be darkened at will.

The *front and/or upper* cabins may give a greater sensation of motion than *lower or rear* cabins. On the other hand, they tend to pick up less engine noise and vibrations.

Make your clients aware of these variances, but don't sell a specific location as the best on the ship. Why might you be tempted to do so? Because clients ask you for the best cabin. If you say, for instance, that the best is midship, outside, then that's what they may decide they want. But what happens if the midship outside cabins are sold out? You have created instant disappointment. The sale takes a dive, possibly to no sale at all. They don't want to spend money for second-rate accommodations.

A better approach to accommodations is, "All the cabins are good. What's best depends on what you prefer. But regardless of your selection, all of the cruise amenities, features, activities, and dining are the same." Then ask them questions to determine what they do prefer. Or give more information about each location and get a reading from them. Take note when they seem interested, and zero in.

ELIMINATING MISGIVINGS ABOUT CRUISING

There are a lot of good things to say about cruising. But not all people are one hundred percent sold on the idea. Some travelers secretly harbor certain fears or reservations. These are usually expressed in the form of an objection. For example, Mr. Vernon says his wife wants to go on a cruise, but he's afraid he'll get bored. There are three things you should do.

1. Do not answer the objection by refuting it, i.e., do not say, "It's really not like that." Acknowledge that you hear the concern, and say, "I understand what you're saying."
2. Let them know others have felt this way.
3. Explain why the fear is unfounded.

The most common misgivings, or fears, about cruising are:

- Boredom
- Confinement

- Seasickness

- Drowning

- Navy service

There are a number of ways to explain why these fears are unfounded:

Boredom. Emphasize the number and variety of scheduled onboard activities, as well as the opportunities to go ashore and explore. (Put people who fear boredom on a cruise that makes the most stops in a given time period.)

Confinement. Emphasize the size of the ships and the freedom of movement as among its many attractions. (Put people who fear confinement on a larger ship and in a larger cabin. Underscore the fact that they have choices.)

Seasickness. Emphasize the fact that the ships use stabilizers to reduce and virtually eliminate roll. Mention that there is a doctor on board. Tell them that Dramamine and the Transderm Scōp patch can counter impending motion sickness. Mention that ships reroute to avert storms and rough seas. (Put people who fear seasickness on a cruise that sails close to land, as opposed to one that sails in open sea. Choose one that cruises the Bahamas instead of from New York to Bermuda.)

Drowning. Assure them that there is a life jacket for each passenger, and that a mandatory lifeboat drill is held as they leave their port of embarkation. Point out that high, sturdy railings enclose all open deck space.

Navy. Remind them that, unlike the navy, on cruise ships there are no whistles and bells telling them when to get up, when to go to sleep, or anyone giving them orders. They'll have a private room and bath, and they can party and dance the night away if they wish.

HELPING CLIENTS CHOOSE A CRUISE SHIP

In order to help your clients choose a cruise ship, you must know your cruise products and suppliers. Be aware that each cruise line distinguishes itself from its competitors by establishing a market niche. Some gear themselves to a particular people market; for example, women over fifty-five, families with children, or students. Others may use a product niche, that is, they combine a cruise with land packages for one price. Still others compete by specializing in geographic areas, such as the Amazon River, the Nile River, or the Norwegian fjords. There are even lines that offer educational cruises that specialize in, for example, nature, history, culture, archaeology, and remote areas accessible only by ship. You must be familiar not only with a typical seven-day Caribbean excursion, but also with a barge trip on the canals of France, a paddle wheel voyage on the Mississippi River, a yacht journey in the Greek Islands, a point-to-point ferry ride up Alaska's Inside Passage, and a vacation on a ship so large that it sells itself as the destination.

You must be able to advise your clients about cruise durations, ports of call, and prices. You must describe such things as nationality of the staff and size of the vessel. You must also be familiar with the character of the ships: study the brochure and feel free to get the cruise reservationist's opinion about the ship's atmosphere. Is it sedate or noisy? Is it formal or casual? Does it remind one of an adult camp or a rest home? Does the entertainment lean toward big bands and instrumental music or discos and flashing lights? Does the ship offer singalongs or operas? Is the decor elegant or pop? Are the meals haute cuisine or homestyle? Black tie or jeans for dinner?

You must know, too, about the itineraries of the ships. Is the ship strongly promoting destinations? Is the itinerary port-intensive, or does it depend more on at-sea activities? Do the ports offer a variety of scenery or activities, or are they all quite similar? Does the ship cruise in the daytime because scenery is the primary attraction, such as a Rhine River cruise, and dock at night for evening entertainment in the city? Or does it cruise at night when there's nothing to see, like some cruises in the Caribbean, and dock all day in a port where there is much to see and do?

All this information can be accumulated by studying brochures (note the age of the travelers in the pictures, the way they are dressed, and the level of their activity), attending cruise seminars, exchanging information with other agents, and talking with cruise reservationists. And, of course, by going on cruises yourself!

WORKING WITH THE CRUISE RESERVATIONIST

Once clients commit to reserve a cabin on a cruise, it is advisable to book the space immediately while the clients are still at your desk or on the phone. This allows less time for the clients to change their minds, and also saves you time because if any changes need to be made (e.g., their preferred space is not available) or questions answered, you can do it right away and get on to the next item. Otherwise, you face call-backs, busy lines, answering machines, and possible loss of space because of indecision and lag time.

In working with cruise reservationists, remember that they work to sell space for the cruise line. This means that they have to sell the least desirable cabins as well as the most desirable. You, on the other hand, work to satisfy your clients. Therefore, stand firm to get what you want.

> Counsellor: "I'd like to book on the *Sea Mermaid*, July 21, cabin B52 or the vicinity, double bed, for two adults."

Let's say that this space is midship outside, second passenger deck.

> Reservationist: "I can give you cabin B7."
>
> Counsellor: "Do you have something more midship near cabin B52?"

If your original request is not available, the reservationist may try to get you to buy a cabin that is more difficult to sell. If you buy, the reservationist is happy. The better space can be sold to more demanding agents. Be that demanding agent. If you don't like the offer, ask again for better space. Many times, you'll get it. If you don't get a cabin closer to your preference on the second push, then a closer cabin just isn't available. Take what the reservationist offers. You are always better off taking an offer and waitlisting the preferred space than hesitating and calling back later, when even the alternate space may not be available.

GETTING DISCOUNTED SPACE

Most cruise lines offer cabins at prices below listed brochure rates. These discounted prices are offered through travel agents in three ways: 1) advance booking discounts, 2) guarantees, and 3) supersavers or seasavers. Check directly with each line to determine who offers what at the time you are selling cruises.

Advanced booking discounts. Many lines offer passengers a discount if they either book a certain length of time in advance of the sailing, and/or pay a certain amount by a specific time. Brochures advertise this type of discount on the cover or on the pages of price listings. Your clients need to decide whether they prefer to keep their money in the bank collecting interest, or if the discount is great enough to let the cruise line have the money six months or more in advance.

Guarantees. A guarantee is an assurance by a cruise line that, for a stated price, the client will receive a cabin in that price group, or a *more expensive cabin,* by agreeing to take any cabin in either group, at the cruise line's discretion. In essence, the clients are gambling that they will get a more expensive cabin than what they are paying for. In almost all cases, they do. On the down side, however, they don't know which cabin they'll get until just prior to sailing. And although overall the cabin may be better, they may not get the location or bed arrangement they prefer and would have had if they had booked a specific cabin.

So if you have clients who are flexible about cabin size, location, bed arrangement, and are interested in a good financial arrangement, a guarantee is usually a good deal. But if they must have a double bed or an outside window and do not want to compromise, do not fool with a guarantee. Book a specific cabin for these clients.

The cruise line can offer a guarantee at any time and in any category, and the offer can fluctuate by the hour. The line can also withdraw it at any time. They offer guarantees to top off space, to secure a booking that is in jeopardy because requested space is not available, or to fill cancelled cabins quickly. When these conditions no longer exist, they stop offering guarantees. Keep in mind that guarantees are not advertised. And often reservationists will not volunteer that they are available—they prefer first to try to sell the cabins at full price. You can find out only by asking.

Let's say you request a cabin in category four, which is entirely sold out. In order not to jeopardize the sale, the reservationist then says, "I can give you a confirmed cabin in category five or a guarantee in category four." If your clients are flexible, grab the offer. If the reservationist does not offer a guarantee as an alternative, ask, "Can you give me a guarantee in category four?"

Supersavers. A few lines advertise supersavers, discounted rates offered within thirty days of any sailing. Unlike the advance discounts and guarantees, these offers are not for a specific ship or sailing date and do not include air fare. One flat rate is charged for any inside cabin, regardless of whether it has bunk beds or a king-sized bed, a standard cabin or a suite, or any other variable. A slightly higher flat rate is charged for any outside cabin—again, regardless of variables.

The clients' only choice is the weekend they want to cruise and whether they want an inside or outside cabin. The cruise line decides everything else, including the ship, the day of sailing, and the cabin. The total price must be prepaid within a few days after the booking is confirmed. Penalty for cancellation is usually about $200 per person.

Supersavers are for clients who simply want to go on a cruise and to go cheaply. They must be extremely flexible. They may get a ship that goes to St. Thomas where they've been twice already, or they may get a Saturday sailing when they prefer Sunday. They have no choice. The cruise line offers this low rate in order to top off cabin space that has not sold at regular price.

COMPLETING THE PAPERWORK

After you complete the booking with the supplier, collect the required deposit or the full payment from the clients. Then thoroughly explain to them what happens next.

Tell them that you will forward their money to the cruise line. And that when you receive confirmation—usually within fourteen to twenty-one days—you will forward a copy to them. Tell them when final payment is due. Tell them that you will receive the necessary documents—tickets, vouchers, cruise ticket, baggage tags, etc.—about ten days prior to the sailing, and you will notify them when the documents arrive. Now that they know the schedule of events, they won't think something is wrong because they haven't received anything five days after they gave you their money. They will continue to trust you.

When you forward payment to the supplier, include a typed note giving clients' names, ship, sailing date, cabin, confirmation number, price, whether the money represents deposit, final payment or full payment, and any other necessary information. Be specific; this avoids problems. If you don't include a cover note saying what the payment is for, write the information on the back of the check. Be sure to note in your records the amounts paid in and paid out, and the dates.

If the documents do not arrive by the date you expect, give the cruise line a call right away. We are all human and mistakes are made. Prevent a minor one from getting out of hand. Check on what's happening when there's still time to correct any problems.

When you *do* receive the documents, go over them before you call the client to say they've arrived. If there is an error, call the company right away. (*Hint*: If you ever have to send documents back to the cruise line, send only the essentials. Keep the baggage tags and information booklets.)

When clients come in for the documents, go over each voucher and piece of paper. They don't know what they're supposed to have. It's up to you to tell them, and to tell them clearly, what to do with each piece of paper. If you mail the documents, call your clients first and go over them. If your clients have questions after they receive their documents, ask them to call you back.

Cruise Ship Atlantic
Photo: Courtesy Home Lines Cruises, Inc.

REVIEW

SET 1

1. Who goes on cruises? _____

_____

_____

2. Give four selling points for cruising.

_____

_____

_____

_____

3. What is a guarantee on a cruise ship?

_____

_____

_____

_____

4. When clients book supersaver rates they get to choose which of the following as part of the deal:

_____ a. airline seats, sailing date, specific cabin

_____ b. cruise weekend dates, general inside or outside location for a cabin

_____ c. cruise weekend dates, specific cabin, ship

_____ d. type of bed, date of sailing

151

SET 2

1. How do cruises differ?

_____

_____

_____

2. How do you guide someone in the selection of meal sittings?

_____

_____

_____

_____

_____

3. Why should you sell the idea of cruising before you sell a specific ship or itinerary?

_____

_____

_____

_____

4. Why is it inadvisable to promote a specific cabin location as the best, or to encourage clients to buy a particular cabin?

_____

_____

_____

_____

_____

SET 3

1. The clients want to cruise as cheaply as possible, but demand a double bed. They say it doesn't matter where they go because they've never been anywhere. What can you do to try to accommodate them?

   _____

   _____

   _____

2. Client: "When we get to St. Maarten do you think we should go on one of the shore excursions?" Respond.

   _____

   _____

   _____

3. Client: "I'd like to take a cruise; I've heard such wonderful things about vacationing that way. But I'm afraid I'll feel claustrophobic." Respond.

   _____

   _____

   _____

4. Client: "There's a $200 per person difference between the inside and outside cabin. That's an awfully expensive window! I don't think I'd look out the window that much. So just book me something inside." Respond.

_____

_____

_____

_____

12

PREPARING CLIENTS FOR A TRIP

KEY TERMS
Jet Lag
Foreign Currency Dealer

Regardless of where and when your clients go, or how they travel, as a counsellor you owe it to them to prepare them for the trip. How much time you spend on it, though, is a judgment you will need to make depending on the travelers' experience and their destination, and on your agency's counselling policies. Even a few words of encouragement and direction can give travelers a positive attitude and prompt them to make the most of their vacation time.

ADVISING CLIENTS HOW TO TRAVEL SMART

ADOPTING THE RIGHT ATTITUDE

Vacationing is a skill that is learned, and learning any skill begins with the proper mental attitude. Invest a little time to teach your clients some good attitudes about traveling to complement the work you've done matching them with the products. For starters, remind clients that they are leaving home when they travel. This may sound like very basic advice, but a trip can be quickly ruined if the travelers expect a little bit of home when they are in a different part of the United States or in a

155

foreign land and find out they can't get grits, a king-sized bed, or people who can speak English.

And when they are "somewhere else," they are a guest in that place. They should keep this in mind and not be condescending or critical.

A pleasant way to remind your clients of these good attitudes is simply to include a copy of the following with their documents.

THE ART OF TRAVELING (Author Unknown)

When you pack your bags to explore the beauties of your own country or to travel around the world, consider these keys to a happy journey.

Travel lightly. You are not traveling for people to see you.

Travel expectantly. Every place you visit is like a surprise package to be opened. Untie the strings with an expectation of high adventure.

Travel hopefully. "To travel hopefully," wrote Robert Louis Stevenson, "is better than to arrive."

Travel humbly. Visit people and places with reverence and respect for their traditions and ways of life.

Travel courteously. Consideration for your fellow travelers and your hosts will smooth the way through the most difficult days.

Travel gratefully. Show appreciation for the many things that are being done by others for your enjoyment and comfort.

Travel with an open mind. Leave your prejudices at home.

Travel with curiosity. It is not how far you go, but how deeply you go that mines the gold of experience. Thoreau wrote a big book about tiny Walden Pond.

Travel with imagination. As the old Spanish proverb puts it, "He who would bring home the wealth of the Indies, must carry the wealth of the Indies with him."

Travel fearlessly. Banish worry and timidity; the world and its people belong to you just as you belong to the world.

Travel relaxed. Make up your mind to have a good time.

Travel patiently. It takes time to understand others, especially when there are barriers of language and customs; keep flexible and adaptable to all situations.

Travel with the spirit of a world citizen. You'll discover that people are basically much the same the world around. Be an ambassador of good will to all people.

ADVICE ON PACKING

There are plenty of pamphlets and videos available that give lengthy suggestions on what to pack and how to pack. However, clients do appreciate a few words from you. Here are some quick suggestions to pass on to your clients about wardrobe and packing.

Advise your clients to pack half the amount of clothes and twice the amount of money they think they will need for the trip.

Describe the normal weather conditions for the time of year they will be traveling so they take the proper clothing for their destination.

Make a few specific suggestions pertaining to their destination, such as, "Since you are traveling in Asia, remember that laundries are cheap and quick, and clothing is inexpensive. So consider taking a minimal amount of clothing and buying a suitcase there to fill with your purchases."

Make suggestions about packing in relationship to their method of travel. For instance, if they are riding the trains in Europe, strongly suggest that they pack light and use shoulder bags because they will be carrying those bags themselves and will have to lift them above their seats in the train compartment. Luggage with wheels does not work well on cobblestone streets and uneven pavement.

Advise them of any particular dress customs they should observe at the destination and of any particular items to bring that will be helpful. For instance, if they are going to Tahiti tell them to bring an old pair of tennis shoes so they can walk on the coral reefs more easily and without cutting their feet.

Propose that they color coordinate their wardrobe so clothes can be easily mixed and matched, thus requiring them to bring fewer items. White shows dirt quickly; suggest beige instead.

Suggest that they select clothing that can be worn in layers in cooler weather and taken off item by item when the weather turns warmer as the day progresses.

Suggest putting all cosmetics and lotions in small plastic containers. They should squeeze the container when putting the cap on to create suction to avoid leakage at high altitudes.

Alaska
Photo: Courtesy Alaska Division of Tourism/Mark Skok

Suggest that they roll clothes instead of folding, to avoid wrinkles. (And you can get more in the suitcase if you have to!) Tell them to roll items that wrinkle around nonwrinkable ones, and to stuff underwear and socks in shoes.

Suggest that they balance heavy and light items so the suitcase does not topple over.

Advise them to pack in carry-on luggage only those items that they will need in the next twenty-four hours or that are irreplaceable.

Suggest that people traveling independently walk for about half a mile with their packed luggage. If they finish the walk feeling irritated, frustrated, worn out, or achy, tell them to repack their suitcases with different items and/or in a different way, or to use different suitcases.

ADVICE ON MOTION SICKNESS

If any of your clients think they might suffer air or motion sickness during cruise, airplane, car, or train travel, suggest they take Dramamine or bonine, popular brands of antihistamines. Or suggest they talk to their doctor about Transderm Scōp, the patch that is placed behind the ear like a bandaid about four hours prior to when they think they might get sick.

Here are some bits of advice you can pass on to customers who think they might get motion sickness:

- Relax. Tension causes an upset stomach.

- Keep eyes focused on the horizon.

- Drink water *slowly*. And do not put too much liquid in the stomach at one time.

- Do not read.

- On an airplane, sit over the wheels, a position that is more stable.

- Avoid unpleasant odors; stay where there is a flow of air; on an airplane, be sure to keep the air vent open above the seat.

ADVICE ON JET LAG

Jet lag is a physical condition some travelers experience when the body receives mixed signals about what to do when. We are routinely programmed to get up in the morning, eat breakfast, lunch, and dinner at certain times, and sleep during certain hours.

When we fly long distances that cross time zones, our bodies say that four to five hours after eating dinner we're ready for sleep, but according to the clock on the airplane it's time for dinner again. The body gets confused and doesn't function well. Some people feel nauseated; others get headaches. Most suffer from dehydration. Often, there is disorientation, lethargy, drowsiness and sleeplessness at the wrong times, and a "hungover" feeling. Other symptoms are diminished alertness, impaired coordination and strength, and inability to concentrate. Here are suggestions to pass on to customers to help them avoid jet lag:

- Diet. Feast-fast-feast-fast. On the fourth day before flying, eat foods rich in protein and carbohydrates, such as eggs for breakfast and a spaghetti dinner. On the third day prior to flying, eat light food such as soups and salads. On the second day, eat protein and carbohydrates again, and on the day before departure, eat lightly. Avoid caffeine and alcohol. On the day before the flight, drink at least eight 8-ounce glasses of water.

- During the flight. 1) Drink plenty of juice and water; no alcohol, caffeine, or carbonated beverages. 2) Exercise. Move legs up and down; make circles with your ankles; go to the back of the plane and stretch; walk around. 3) Apply lotion regularly to the parts of the body not covered by clothing, such as hands and face.

- Upon arrival. Immediately adopt the time frame of the new destination. If it's morning when you arrive, don't go to bed and sleep as if it were night; stay up and do daytime activities. If you're exhausted upon arrival, wash up, lie down and rest for an hour, and then go out. Wait until evening to go to bed. If it's nighttime when you arrive, go to bed. Even if you don't sleep, just rest quietly. Get up when it's morning.

Many experienced travelers report that a strategy for reducing the discomfort of jet lag is a stopover for two or three days at a point midway between their origin and destination. This gives the body's internal clock time to make the adjustment to the change in schedule at a more reasonable pace.

ADVICE ON SAFETY PRECAUTIONS

You can obtain many books and pamphlets from the government and private companies for customers who are particularly concerned about global safety. But here are a few general precautions to pass on to anyone flying.

- Prior to flight. Don't loiter outside the secured area. Go through security as soon as possible. Never carry anything through security or onto the plane for someone you don't know. In the waiting area, do not sit near trash cans, large expanses of glass, unattended luggage, the check-in counter, or unmarked doors. Do not have your name/address label dangling on the outside of your suitcase. Tape it to the bottom and on the inside.

- On the plane. If traveling in volatile areas, do not carry business cards, political party cards, or the like; pack them. Sit near the window.

- At the destination. Look like you know what you are doing. Walk close to walls in the daytime and away from walls at night. Dress down. Don't wear good jewelry (or even fake jewelry) and expensive clothes that might be out of place. Walk against the flow of pedestrians to discourage anyone from following you, especially as you leave a bank.

ADVISING CLIENTS ABOUT INTERNATIONAL MONEY MATTERS

Your customers often want your advice on carrying and using money while on their trip. As a counsellor, it is your responsibility to provide them with this information.

They can use U.S. cash, U.S. travelers checks, foreign currency travelers checks, foreign cash, and credit cards. Which is best and how much should be carried depends on the individual, the destination, and the type of trip. The following guidelines will help you make recommendations to clients.

CASH

Advise travelers to carry some U.S. cash. How much depends on the destination. Some countries have a higher exchange value for hard cash than for checks or credit cards. People in some countries prefer tips or small gifts in U.S. cash.

It is advisable to purchase some local currency prior to departure so that it can be used upon arrival for bus, taxi, train ride, or a bite to eat. This is especially true if travelers will be arriving late at night when airport exchanges may not be open, or if they are visiting smaller or less traveled areas, where the exchange booths are open only for limited hours.

CHECKS

Recommend that travelers convert the bulk of their spending money into travelers checks. If they are lost or stolen, travelers can report the loss and recoup the funds. These checks have no time limitation and can be cashed any time. There is a fee for purchasing U.S. travelers checks. When they are exchanged for foreign currency there is usually another fee. To avoid double fees and two exchanges, suggest that prior to departure travelers exchange their U.S. money directly into foreign currency travelers checks, provided the exchange rate is reasonable, thus requiring only one exchange and one fee. This can be done through a U.S. foreign currency dealer, such as Reusch International or Deak International, both of whom have 800 phone numbers. For example, let's say your client is going to England. The local currency is the pound sterling (UK£). Have your client fill out the dealer's form specifying the amount of money to be converted and the denominations desired. The client then gives the agency the required cash amount plus the dealer's fee. The agency in turn sends its check to the foreign currency dealer, who sends back the travelers checks in UK£. With these local currency checks on hand upon arrival, the traveler won't have to make an exchange or pay a fee. The checks can be cashed directly in a restaurant, store, or hotel.

When your customers do need to make an exchange in foreign places, advise them that banks are the best place to do so. Hotels usually have an exchange booth, but the rate of exchange *may* not be as favorable as a bank. Travelers can also exchange at money exchange booths in most towns. However, they should beware of making exchanges on the street with the black market or the parallel market. These street exchanges exist in the less politically and economically stable countries. The exchange rates these vendors offer are better than the banks, but often are illegal, and the traveler could be fined or jailed for dealing with them.

CREDIT CARDS

Advise clients to bring at least two different credit cards, since one credit card company may not be accepted everywhere. The advantage in using a credit card abroad is that often several months pass before the traveler receives the bill. However, there are also some disadvantages. One, the exchange rate often is not as good as with cash or checks, and two, even though it may be months before the client receives the bill, the exchange rate by then may be higher than when the purchase was made.

So clients won't actually pay *more* when using a card, tell them to 1) ask what the exchange rate is before using the card, and if they don't like the rate, to use cash; and 2) have the exchange rate written on all copies of the charge receipt so no one can tamper with the rate.

CARRYING MONEY

Regardless of how safe or unsafe a country is, a person is often less careful about keeping track of money while traveling because of a combination of jet lag, fatigue, and new surroundings. This results in carelessness and recklessness. Remind your clients to safeguard their money from the very beginning of the trip to avoid mishaps. Men should carry money in the inside breast pocket of their jackets and, in high crime areas, fastened with a safety pin. If the man is not wearing a jacket, he should use side pockets closed with a pin. Women should carry valuables in shoulder purses with zippered closings, with the strap across the front of the body. For everyone, an even safer method for carrying valuables, day or night, is in a money belt, worn around the waist or neck under the clothing.

Japanese Girl Playing the Shamisen
Photo: Courtesy Japan Air Lines

REVIEW

1. What is jet lag?

_____

_____

_____

2. What five forms of money can travelers consider taking on a foreign trip?

_____

_____

_____

_____

3. What are the advantages of having travelers checks issued in foreign currency?

_____

_____

_____

4. Clients leave New York at 9:15 P.M. on an overnight flight to Lisbon, Portugal. They arrive in Lisbon at 6:15 A.M. For their first day in Lisbon, you recommend that they

_____ a. sleep, since they were awake all night

_____ b. take a six-hour tour of the city since they have all day

_____ c. rest briefly, then spend the day at a leisurely pace

SET 2

1. Demonstrate and describe how money should be carried by men and women when traveling.

   _____

   _____

   _____

   _____

   _____

2. Why might travelers end up paying more when they charge items on a credit card? Do you have any suggestions to help travelers avoid an overcharge?

   _____

   _____

   _____

   _____

SET 3

1. Clients: "Last year we went to the Caribbean. We'd ask for clean towels and they would be delivered six hours later. No one on the island was very service-oriented. Anyway, this year we want to go to Mexico." Do you have any advice for these people?

   _____

   _____

   _____

   _____

   _____

2. Why is it worthwhile for a counsellor to spend some time helping travelers prepare mentally for their trip?

_____

_____

_____

_____

_____

_____

_____

13

FOLLOW-UP SALES

KEY TERMS
Repeat Clients
Referral Clients

The more repeat and referral clients you have, the less time you will spend in servicing them, the less time you will have to spend seeking out new customers, and the more profitable vacation counselling will be for you. Of course, if you sell the right place at the right time at the right price to the right person, there's a good chance that person will use your service again. But if a client feels you took the money for the trip and then acted like both of you disappeared from the face of the earth, the person will be less inclined to do repeat business with you, even if you sold a good trip.

GAINING REPEAT BUSINESS

Get in the habit of viewing your time with clients as building a relationship that will last for years, not just until they leave on their trip. Here are a few techniques that will help you secure repeat business.

For starters, use the client's name from time to time. This helps clients feel that you are at least somewhat interested in them, not just in getting their money.

When you deliver the documents and tickets for the vacation, be sure to wish the client a good trip. Let clients know that even though your part of the transaction has been completed, they can still call you anytime (during business hours) for questions and comments.

When a customer compliments you on your work, whether it's during a sale or upon the return from the trip, don't be falsely modest and say, "Oh, it was nothing." That tends to devalue the trip. Instead, simply reply, "Thank you."

Another way to help secure repeat business is to send clients a thank-you letter or welcome-home letter that will be waiting in the mailbox upon their return. This gesture shows that you are concerned that they had a good time and that all went well. Here is a sample letter:

Dear _____

Our sincere thanks for entrusting us with your travel arrangements.

We hope that you had a pleasant journey and that everything was as you expected. At your convenience, we would enjoy hearing about the highlights of your trip.

We hope to counsel you about the many more trips you'll take.

Sincerely,

Likewise, three months or so after clients have returned from a trip, send another letter enticing them to think about their next trip. Enclose a return postcard asking them to indicate what areas they might be interested in next. Then about every six weeks send appropriate brochures or pieces of literature about those particular places or types of trips.

Of course, just because clients return a postcard asking for information on Jamaica doesn't mean they will go next weekend. Though there is a trend toward taking three or four short vacations instead of one long one, vacationers still tend to mull over the details of a prospective trip for weeks or months. But if you stay in touch with those who travel, they will do repeat business with you when they go again. So be persistent and consistent in your follow-ups. Even if you counselled with some people but did not make a sale, follow-up with them is necessary. They may change their minds and use your services after all, or they may simply take that trip later.

By keeping the lines of communication open, you will learn what your returning vacationers thought about their trip. Their responses serve as marketing research about the destination and also give you a better feel for what they like and don't like, so that you will be better able to help them plan their next vacation.

And if people of a certain age group, level of travel sophistication, or market loved the trip, then possibly other people in the same situation will also like it. This information helps you sell to future customers.

GAINING REFERRAL BUSINESS

Just as people with children know other people with children, people who travel know other people who travel. Tap into that source. You've already cultivated some travelers. Use them to get to the people they know.

There are many methods for gaining referral business. Try a few and see which ones work best in your area. One method that has produced good results for a lot of agencies is to send clients a letter asking them if they know of someone who is thinking of taking a trip and could use your travel services. Enclose a postcard for them to return with this person's name, address, and phone number.

Another technique that gets results is to pay present customers a referral fee or to give them a discount on their next vacation each time they refer a fellow traveler to you.

Another way of getting referral business is to give a destination travelogue at your clients' homes. Ask these clients for an invitation list of their traveling friends, including addresses and phone numbers. Ask them to hold the travelogue, but you send out the invitations, you bring the hors d'oeuvres. And, of course, you will do the show. In exchange for your present clients' endorsement, give them a discount on their next trip, or pay for an optional sightseeing excursion or a day's car rental—anything of appropriate value.

Don't forget to ask your clients if they belong to any clubs where you might give a travelogue or talk. Clubs are always looking for speakers. Gear your talk and the products you present to the specific group, whether they are singles, sports-oriented, or seniors. Ask satisfied customers for testimonials about your service and the vacations you've planned for them. Use the quotes in your next agency newsletter or the next printing of your company's brochure. Or, do a direct mail piece to your neighbors and include the quotes. Most people love to see their names in print. Just be sure to get written permission to quote them. Ask them to sign a short, simple form that says they give your agency permission to use their comments for publicity.

REVIEW

SET 1

1. Why should you say to clients, "Have a good trip"?

_____

_____

_____

2. What is the agency's purpose in sending a welcome-home letter?

_____

_____

_____

3. You have contacted a former customer twice during the past six months to suggest a future vacation, and so far have not been able to sell another trip. Why should you continue to contact this person?

_____

_____

_____

_____

_____

SET 2

1. Why is it easier and quicker to sell a repeat or referral client than to one who found you in the telephone book?

_____

_____

_____

_____

_____

_____

2. Name some ways for soliciting referral customers.

_____

_____

_____

_____

_____

_____

3. How can follow-up with returning travelers serve as marketing research to gain future business for the agency?

_____

_____

_____

_____

_____

_____

14
HANDLING COMPLAINTS ABOUT THE VACATION

You've acted professionally throughout your transactions. You've displayed confidence, honesty, and enthusiasm. You are knowledgeable. You've done everything correctly in planning your client's trip. What could possibly go wrong? Well, a lot. Because you don't go on the trips with your clients, you depend on other travel personnel to deliver the products you sold them.

Clients returning from a trip may have a legitimate complaint. Often *you* are expected to rectify the situation because you're the one who sold the trip. Clients may use the ploy of bringing up the relationship between you, and make that the basis for you to handle the complaint. They'll remind you that they've been good customers for years, or that you were recommended. The first thing to say in response to this is to repeat this premise. Say that you do recognize them as good repeat customers. Generally, this is all anyone needs to hear to become calm and reasonable.

LETTING THE CUSTOMER TALK

When a client issues a formal complaint, the first thing to do is treat it with respect regardless of how petty the grievance. The second thing to do is listen. Don't argue with the client, don't denounce the supplier, don't deny your involvement.

On the other hand, however, do not assume automatically that you did something wrong. Wait until responsibility has been established. Don't be defensive. If indeed you are the one at fault, admit it. Don't go to such extremes, though, with your

self-chastisement that the client loses total confidence in your abilities. Keep your head up, make eye contact with the customer, and keep your voice strong yet sincere.

As you listen there are only two things you should be doing:

1. Acknowledge that you are listening with short verbal responses, such as "uh-huh, mmm, oh, right. . . ."
2. Take only *brief* notes.

The main thing that clients want is for you "to care." It's all right to say that you're sorry it happened to them. But avoid saying, "I know how uncomfortable that must have been for you. . . ." You don't; it didn't happen to you. They want their predicament to be *theirs*. Instead say, "I regret that you were uncomfortable."

MAKING AMENDS

COMPLAINTS DURING A TRIP

Sometimes a traveler who has a complaint or a problem while on the trip calls you immediately *collect* to air the grievance or to get a solution. When you receive one of these calls, listen to the problem. Then solve it as best you can. Don't be concerned at this point about *why* there is a problem. Help your client find lost luggage, or get a room, *now,* and worry later about why the luggage was lost, or a room not reserved.

Example: Mr. and Mrs. Phillip Samuels arrive in Cancun, Mexico, with a hotel confirmation in hand. But the hotel says that it does not show their reservation and has no room for them. Mr. Samuels uses the lobby phone to call you. Listen to his explanation of the problem. Stay calm and quiet. Acknowledge that you hear him.

Then tell Mr. Samuels to put the front desk or reservations manager on the phone. Be friendly with this person. Remind the manager that these clients do possess a confirmation slip; tell the manager to find them a room, any room. If friendliness doesn't work, resort to firm words. If the response is that there simply is no room at the hotel, say that it's the manager's responsibility to walk the clients. The manager pays for the clients' transportation to a comparable hotel, and for their stay there until a room is available at the hotel the clients originally booked.

Once the situation is settled, you can proceed to find out how the difficulty occurred so you can explain it to the clients when they return. Did the deposit get sidetracked so the space was cancelled? Did the hotel's computer dump the record? Did the establishment overbook?

COMPLAINTS AFTER A TRIP

True story: "A client returns from a 15-day first class tour of Europe organized and escorted by a well-known company. Upon contacting the client to see how the

Cancun, Mexico
Photo: Courtesy Mexican Tourist Board

trip went, the agent learns that everything was great until the very end, when the tour escort made a strong hint about 'wanting a good tip,' which turned the passenger sour. A fellow traveler was firmly designated by the escort to collect this tip."

When a complaint is lodged *after* the trip, listen to it, and then ask your client: "Is there anything else I need to know about the situation?" This is an invitation to tell you any hidden problems, and whether the voiced complaint really *is* the complaint. For example, a Club Med traveler may complain about the room, when the real problem was the incompatible roommate.

Once you've heard the real complaint, you can act upon it if there is a clear-cut solution, e.g., a client was double-billed for something and you need to make a refund. If there are several possible solutions to the problem—money can be refunded or a discount given on the next trip—state them to the client and ask which is preferred. If the problem remains unclear, complicated, or truly damaging to the point that liability seems likely to result, ask the client to put the details in writing. This assures greater accuracy. The details, along with your cover letter, are then forwarded to the supplier. At this point, if the matter is largely between the client and the supplier, you should limit your involvement. Just support your client as necessary.

Even if the client's complaint appears so petty that it doesn't deserve any action, ask that the details be put in writing; often the client won't bother. If it does happen, simply write a cover letter supporting the customer, and send it all to the supplier. This way you have displayed your loyalty to the customer without jeopardizing productivity.

When the solutions are to come from the supplier and not from you, e.g., the client paid for a tour on an air-conditioned sightseeing bus and the air-conditioning did not work and was not replaced, start by lodging the complaint with the supplier and ask for compensation. All the client may require is a letter of apology from the supplier.

But if the traveler expects and deserves greater compensation, whether it's money, a discount on a future trip, or a free item from the supplier, it may become a matter of negotiation. In this case, you want a win/win situation wherein both parties will be satisfied with the outcome. Start by asking for the most you can hope for as compensation, but be realistic in what you ask. If there is a disagreement, be diplomatic. Value your supplier's position. Attacks are not productive. Neither is idly threatening that you won't use that company again. If you have been a satisfied repeat customer of the supplier, you don't want to risk the rapport between you because of one incident. It takes time to build relationships. If an incident occurs with your first booking and you have no track record of frequent business with the supplier, there is no guarantee how much business you really would have done there in the future.

So when you disagree, be fair, but firm, and say, "I realize that as an experienced tour company, you cannot take seriously every little frustration. But considering the length of time my client had to endure the lack of air-conditioning, it would be fair to refund half the money."

REVIEW

SET 1

1. What is the first thing you do when a client has a complaint?

   _____

2. What is usually the main thing that a client who voices a complaint wants from you?

   _____

   _____

   _____

3. What is your first line of action after you listen to a client who is calling you collect concerning a problem?

   _____

   _____

   _____

4. What question can you ask clients to find out whether they are telling you their complaints or genuine concerns about a trip?

   _____

   _____

SET 2

1. When is it a good idea to get the complaint in writing from the traveler?

   _____

   _____

   _____

2. How should you act if you're the one who caused the problem?

_____

_____

_____

3. If there are several solutions to a problem, should you

_____ a. choose one

_____ b. state the solutions and ask which the client prefers

_____ c. take the cheapest and quickest way out

_____ d. deal with the problem later

SET 3

1. A client returns from a trip and brings you a long letter detailing a complaint about the food that was served at group meals. The client hands you the letter and says, "Take care of this." What should you do?

_____

_____

_____

_____

_____

_____

_____

_____

INDEX